THE 1
HORSE

CAMBRIDGESHIR

AVAILABLE IN THIS SERIES

The Cotswolds on Horseback
Wiltshire on Horseback
Westmorland on Horseback
The Ridgeway Downs on Horseback
Exmoor on Horseback
Somerset on Horseback
Hampshire on Horseback
Leicestershire & Rutland on Horseback
Humberside on Horseback
Northamptonshire on Horseback
Dorset on Horseback
Cambridgeshire on Horseback

First published 1996
by The British Horse Society
Access & Rights of Way Department
British Equestrian Centre
Stoneleigh Park, Kenilworth
Warwickshire CV8 2LR

A catalogue record for this book is available from
the British Library

ISBN 1 899016 09 0

Printed by:
Tripod Press Limited, 7 Wise Street, Leamington Spa, CV31 3AP

Distribution:
The British Horse Society, Stoneleigh Park, Kenilworth,
Warwickshire, CV8 2LR

CONTENTS

ACKNOWLEDGEMENTS

A number of people and organisations have given their time and expertise to provide details for this book, or contributed in some other material way.

In particular the British Horse Society would like to thank Susan, Roger, Laura and Hannah Reynolds and their ponies 'Becci' and 'Pippin', Mrs Gwen Riley; Sue Jeggo, Lesley Boyle, Rebecca Jackson, Sue Thorogood, Derek Saunders, David and Elaine Abercrombie and Michael Brown for surveying, developing and describing the routes; Sue Smith and 'Dilly', Katie Duff and 'Music' for test riding the routes; Isabelle Reid and her ponies and John Meadows for the cover photographs; Kerstin Alford for her excellent illustrations and Alison Hodges, Assistant Rights of Way Officer, Cambridgeshire County Council, for her help and support. We would also like to thank John Bennett who, supported by his wife Brenda and daughter Kirsten, surveyed, developed, described and walked nine of the trails in the book and then went on to fill them with interesting details.

Finally, thanks to Philippa Luard and Elwyn Hartley Edwards for their literary contributions.

FOREWORD

When the British Horse Society launched its ARROW Project in 1991, few people could have foreseen the tremendous response and commitment that it would provoke from recreational drivers and riders. That eight trail guide books were in print by May 1994 with the prospect of a further eight in 1995, is testament to their dedication and talent. I am delighted, on behalf of all equestrians, to pay tribute to those who have made such a unique contribution towards the achievement of a network of circular and linear trails.

The Society is concerned that little had been achieved for carriage drivers within ARROW: however it is pleasing that some progress has now been made and that a number of driving trails will be featured this year and in subsequent years.

It is a fact that drivers are restricted to Byways and Unclassified County Road, thus there are fewer chances to provide them with off-road driving opportunities. This calls for a separate approach, with our Rights of Way staff and volunteers working hand-in-glove with drivers and driving organisations, in order to identify and claim lost routes. The Access & Rights of Way Policy Committee, in overseeing this initiative, will do all in its power to gain maximum benefit for drivers from this important partnership.

As it is virtually impossible to produce a circular or linear route without incorporating some metalled highways it is difficult to lay claim to having opened up a given mileage of 'off-road' riding.

What can be claimed however, is that by the end of 1995 details of up to 350 trails, totalling about 5000 miles, should be in print.

With a further eight books planned for 1996/97 and others in prospect towards the millennium, the Society can, with some justification, feel proud to have contributed to the safety and the greater enjoyment of those who take pleasure from riding and carriage driving.

E A T BONNOR-MAURICE
Chairman, British Horse Society

PREFACE

Conditioned as we are to the spread of urban development and its supportive system of trunk roads that encroach, inevitably, upon the countryside, it comes as a surprise to reflect that for well over a thousand years after the withdrawal of the Roman legions no public roads were built in britain, much less new towns and industrial centres. Indeed, the Romans legacy of 5000 miles (8,000 km) of surfaced via strata did not long survive the departure of its builders. Its lapse into decay was to all intents synonymous with the decline and ultimate eclipse of the beleaguered empire itself.

It was not until 1780 that the system of toll roads had reached that figure again. Fifty years later, thanks principally to the efforts of Telford and McAdam, Britain had 20,000 miles (32,000 km) of good roadways underpinning what became known as the Golden Age of Coaching.

Within the past half-century that road system and the myriad acres of developed areas it services has been multiplied more than a hundred times over, whilst the open countryside and, in consequence, the means of access to it, has been eroded commensurately.

Up to the Industrial Revolution and for many years thereafter, the countryside was crisscrossed with tracks, some of them dating from prehistoric times and other relics of the Roman occupation. They provided trade routes for the transport of every sort of commodity as well as being an essential facility for the traveller. John Wesley, for instance, who led the Methodist revival of the 19th century, reckoned to ride 8000 miles on such tracks in the course of a year. There was, also a comprehensive system of long-distance drove roads, the equivalent of our modern road system, over which thousands and thousands of cattle, sheep, pigs, geese and turkeys were driven to the main centres of population (cattle were shod for the journey and even geese had their webbed feet protected by a pad of tar and sawdust).

The land enclosures of the 18th and 19th centuries took an obvious toll of all kinds of previously public routes and industrial development, dependent on railways, roads and canals, made further inroads into the public rights of access. After that the intensification of farming practice and the sheer speed and scope of urban building were both factors in breaking up the old network of tracks lanes and paths.

Nonetheless, it was possible, just fifty years ago, for Aime Tschiffely, the archetypal long-distance rider who described his 10,000 mile (16,000 km) two and a half year journey from Buenos Aires to Washington DC in his classic The Tales of Two Horses, to take a 'leisurely jaunt' through England on horseback. The book of that 'jaunt' was called simply Bridle Paths and the idea, he said, was to 'jog along, anyhow and anywhere; canter along quiet country lanes, over hills and through dales - sunshine or rain - alone with a horse to see the real England' and he could have done the same in Scotland or Wales.

Twenty years after Tschiffely, the broadcaster Wynford Vaughan Thomas made a TV programme of a ride from one end of Wales to the other over the upland ways once traversed by the sad and shadowy princes of that country. Some of those historic routes are no longer open to horsemen, but Wales can still boast the Pilgrim's Ride, the route followed by the devout in their pilgrimage to Bardsey, the island of the Saints, as well as Glyndwr's Way which traverses the most rugged of the upland country. Elsewhere there are other long-distance routes, the South Downs Way, the Pennine and so on, whilst there still remain many shorter routes all over the country that provide the basis for our modern public paths.

Most prominent and active within the environmental lobby seeking to extend and protect the right of off-road riders is the British Horse Society's Access and Rights of Way Committee, co-ordinating the work of over 100 honorary Bridleways Officers in the UK. Amongst its declared objectives, laid down in its National Strategy for Access is 'the establishment of a basic network of public bridleways and byways in all counties, with cross-country and regional links.' It works towards 'linking long distance bridleways in most areas - so that a rider may travel the country if he so desires.'

This handbook with accurate material supplied by local enthusiasts is just one of a series published by the BHS which in the foreseeable future will cover every region of the country, reflecting and reinforcing the need to preserve an invaluable part of our heritage for as long as men and women find their pleasure 'along country lanes, over hills and through dales - sunshine or rain' along with a horse and like-minded companions.

ELWYN HARTLEY EDWARDS

INTRODUCTION

The British Horse Society's ARROW Project aims to identify open and usable routes of varying length and shape (circular, figure-of-eight or linear) to help riders and carriage drivers to enjoy the countryside by means, as far as possible, of the network of public rights of way and the minor vehicular highways. This collection of rides is the result of research and mapping by volunteers who took up the challenge of the ARROW initiative with such enthusiasm and effort.

I am faced with the equally daunting challenge of writing an introductory chapter. Should I write reams about each topic or try simply to point you in the right direction? I have decided upon the second method as the search for information is itself highly educative and stays in the mind better than reading it all in one place. Also, since we all have different expectations of our holiday, a very full guide seemed wrong. Nevertheless, there are a few pointers I would like to suggest to you.

The most important one is to start your planning several months in advance of the trip, including a visit to the area you intend to ride in. You should make endless lists of things to DO (e.g. get the saddle checked) and things to CHECK OUT (can you read a map, for instance). You may find joining the local BHS Endurance Riding Group very helpful, as there you will meet people who can give you information about the degree of fitness needed for yourself and your horse (feeding for fitness not dottiness), and many other useful hints on adventurous riding. You may also enjoy some of the Pleasure rides organised by the group or by the local Riding Club. These are usually about 15-20 miles and you ride in company, though using a map. You

may find them under the title Training Rides. These rides will get both of you used to going into strange country. If you usually ride on well-known tracks, then your horse will find it nerve-racking to go off into new territory, and you yourself may also find the excitement of deep country a bit surprising, so try to widen your experience at home before you go off on holiday.

ACCOMMODATION

Decide how far you wish to ride each day of your holiday, book overnight accommodation for both of you and if possible visit it to see if the five-star suite on offer to your horse is what he is used to. Decide if you want to stable him or to turn him out at the end of the day, and arrange to drop off some food for him, as he will not relish hard work on a diet of green grass, nor will he enjoy a change in his usual food. If you are to have a back-up vehicle, of course, then you will not need to do some of this, but you should certainly make a preliminary visit if you can. The BHS publish a Bed & Breakfast Guide for Horses which is a list of people willing to accommodate horses, and sometimes riders, overnight. The Society does not inspect these places, so you should check everything in advance.

FITNESS

You and your horse should be fit. For both of you , this is a process taking about two months. If you and/or your horse are not in the full flush of youth, then it may take a bit longer. The office chair, the factory floor, or the household duties do not make or keep you fit, but carefully planned exercise will. Remember that no matter how fit your horse seems, he does not keep himself fit - you get him fit. There are several books with details of fitness programmes for a series of rides. Do not forget to build in a rest day during your holiday - neither of you can keep going all the time, day after day. Miles of walking may get you fit, but it uses different muscles from riding; you may get a surprise when you start riding longer distances. It seems to me that the further you intend to ride, the longer your preparation should be. Nothing can be done in a hurry.

Your horse should be obedient, so work on that. If you want him to stand, then he must stand. If you want to go through water, then he must be prepared to walk down a slope or even step down off a bank to go through the stream, so start with puddles and insist that he go through the middle. Does he help you open gates? I hope so, or you will have a great deal of mounting and dismounting to do. Does he tie up - this is essential if you are to have a peaceful pint at lunchtime.

MAPS

Can you read a map? Can you make and read a grid reference (usually referred to as GR)? Get a Pathfinder map of your area and take yourself for a walk and see if you end up where you expect to. Learn to know exactly where you are on the map, and how to understand the symbols (if your map shows hilly ground, the journey will take longer). Can you work out how long a ride is in miles and roughly how long it will take? You will be using rights of way and it is very important that you stay in the line of the path - that is the only place you have a right to be, and you may deviate from that line only as much as is necessary to get you round an obstruction on the path. You are going to be riding over land that forms part of someone's work place and that fact must be respected.

It is only by the efforts of farmers and landowners that the countryside exists in its present form - so that we may enjoy it as we pass by.

You will need to know the grid reference (GR.) of the start and end of the various tracks you are to use. Get a copy of an Ordnance Survey (OS) Landranger map and really learn the details on the right-hand side, some of which explain how to arrive at a Grid Reference. Learn to go in the door (Eastings - from left to right) and up the stairs (Northings - from bottom to top). There is a great deal of information on the Landranger maps and not so much on the Pathfinders, but the Pathfinder gives more details on the map itself, so that is the map you will use for the actual ride. Or you may care to buy a Landranger of the area you are visiting and, using a highlighter pen, mark in all the rides you want to make, so that you can see through the marks you make. Then get from any Outdoor shop a map case which will allow you to read the map without taking it out of the case and which you can secure round yourself. Also, you should know if you are facing north, south, east or west as you ride. Quite important if you think about it, as it is no good riding into the sunset if you are meant to be going south. Plastic orienteering compasses are cheap and reliable.

TACK

Have your tack thoroughly checked by your saddler, as there is nothing so annoying as a sore back which could have been prevented, or an unnecessarily broken girth strap. How are you going to carry the essential headcollar and rope each day? What about spare shoes, or a false shoe?

What to take on the ride depends on how much back-up you have. If you have to carry a change of clothes, etc., then you are into very careful planning indeed - balance saddle bag, the lot. If you are based at your first night stop all the time, then life is much easier. You should always carry a first aid kit for horse and rider. You will also have to plan how to wash the girth and numnah. Remember our delightful climate and always carry a waterproof and additional warm clothing - it never pays to gamble with rain and wind.

SAFETY

It is always wiser to ride in company. The other person can always hold your horse, or pull you out of the ditch, as well as being someone to talk to about the excitements of the day and to help plan everything. You should always wear a BSI riding hat, properly secured, and also safe footwear. You need a clearly defined heel and a smooth sole. Even if riding in company, tell someone where you are going and roughly how long you expect to take. If affordable, take a portable telephone. Make a list of the things you must carry every day and check it before leaving base.

INSURANCE

You should have Third Party Legal Liability Insurance. This will protect you if you or your horse cause a bit of mayhem (accidentally!). Membership of the BHS gives you this type of insurance, plus Personal Accident Insurance as part of the membership package. Check your household insurance to make sure it covers riding before you rely only on that, as some insurances do not. You should always have this type of cover when venturing forth into the outside world, even if it is an hours hack from home.

PARKING

If you intend to box to the start of the day's ride, either have someone to take the box away or make sure it is safely,

securely and considerately parked. If you have to make arrangements to park, do it well in advance or the contact may well have gone to market or the hairdressers when you make a last minute call. Have the vehicle number etched on to the windows for security.

MONEY

This is vital, so work out a system of getting money if necessary. Sadly we can no longer gallop up to the bank and lead Dobbin into the cashier's queue, nor do most banks have hitching rails. Post Offices are more numerous and might be a useful alternative. Always have the price of a telephone call on you.

Lastly, if you do run into problems of blocked paths or boggy ones, write to the Highway Authority of the relevant county council and tell them. Then you can do something about it. You might even think of adopting a path near home and keeping an eye on it, telling your own county council of any difficulties you encounter. It is through such voluntary work that these rides have been made possible.

Wherever you ride, always do it responsibly, with care of the land, consideration for the farmer and courtesy for all other users. Remember the Country Code and enjoy your ARROW Riding.

I hope this chapter will have started you planning and making lists. If I seem to be always writing about forward planning it is only because I usually leave things to the last minute, which causes chaos!

PHILIPPA LUARD

CODE FOR RIDING & DRIVING RESPONSIBLY

THE BRITISH
HORSE SOCIETY

1.   **Riders and carriage drivers** everywhere should proceed with courtesy, care and consideration. The British Horse Society recommends the following:

Care for the Land
Do not stray off the line of the path;
Do not damage timber or hedgerows by jumping;
Remember the horses' hooves can damage surfaces in bad weather;
Pay particular attention to protected areas that have significant historical and/or biological value, as they are extremely sensitive to damage.

Courtesy to other users
Remember that walkers, cyclists and other riders may be elderly, disabled, children or simply frightened of horses; whenever possible acknowledge courtesy shown by drivers or motor vehicles.

Consideration for the farmer
Shut the gate behind you;
Ride slowly past all stock;
Do not ride on cultivated land unless the right of way crosses it;
Dogs are seldom welcome on farmland or moorland unless on a lead or under close control.

2.   **Observe local byelaws**

3.   **Ride or drive with care on the roads** and take the BHS Riding and Road Safety Test. Always make sure that you can be seen at night or in bad visibility, by wearing the right kind of reflective/fluorescent aids.

4.   **Groups from riding establishments** should contain reasonable numbers, for reasons of both safety and amenity. They should never exceed twenty in total **including** the relevant number of escorts as indicated in BHS guidelines on levels of capability among riders in groups, available on request. Rides should not deviate from the right of way or permitted route and regard must be shown at all times for growing crops, shutting and securing of gates and the consideration and courtesy due to others.

5.   **Always obey the Country Code in every way possible:**
Enjoy the countryside and respect its life and work
Guard against all risk of fire
Fasten all gates
Keep your dogs under close control
Keep to public paths across farmland
Use gates and stiles to cross fences, hedges and walls
Leave livestock, crops and machinery alone
Take your litter home
Help keep all water clean
Protect wildlife, plants and trees
Take special care on country roads
Make no unnecessary noise.

INTRODUCTION TO CAMBRIDGESHIRE

When you say Cambridgeshire, most people think of either a University town or the Fens.

Much of the county was formerly under water, and about a fifth is below sea level. Most bridleways go back several hundred years, and it is not surprising that much of the county is sparsely provided with them, for until comparatively recently most transport was by boat, and although water carriage has great advantages over land in the ability to carry heavy loads unaffected by rain and snow, unfortunately it provides no legal precedent for rights of way on horseback or on foot. Fortunately, after the great drainage projects of the 17th, 18th and 19th centuries, public roads reached out into the newly-drained agricultural land providing a network of public byways for safe, quiet off-road riding. From the highest point at 254 feet in the Gog Magog Hills just south of Cambridge to the Fens below sea level around Ely, Cambridgeshire provides a diverse landscape for riding.

Horse racing at Newmarket excites hope of equestrian activity, although Newmarket itself is in Suffolk. The July Course and most of the Old Course are, however, in Cambridgeshire, and here may be a clue to the local importance of the horse. Horse racing perhaps started at Newmarket in order to give Charles II an excuse to have a weekend near his mistress, but the real reason is surely that Newmarket Heath lies on the Icknield Way, that great prehistoric track which runs right across England and was the main east-west route for men and animals, by reason of its elevated and dry chalk path. Now restricted to the A505 and A11, it is easy to forget that at one time it was several miles wide, as can be seen from the width of Devil's Dyke and its associated ditches, which barred the way when

built in the Dark Ages, though by whom and for what reason, we are still waiting for the historians and archaeologists to tell us.

The west and south of the county also belies the expectations of flat fen, being rolling and often wooded, although the height of the ground may be no more than 100 to 200 feet. Here one can feel oneself in traditional English countryside with fields, woods and small villages. The fields are surprisingly large and the broad horizons show that the world of the Fens is not far away.

In the north, in the lands of the old Soke of Peterborough, once part of Northamptonshire, the great oolitic limestone belt crosses the county between the rivers Nene and Welland on its journey across England from the Cotswolds to the North York Moors. The geology creates a hilly landscape of ample woods and deeper valleys with stone-built villages.

Here, just inside the county boundary in the shadow of Burghley House, the Burghley Horse Trials take place at the beginning of September in Capability Brown's breathtaking parkland. Near Peterborough, close to the A1, is the East of England Showground - a mecca for equestrian activities with events like the Shire Horse Show, Ponies (UK), the BSPS Championships and the East of England Show itself, drawing horselovers to Cambridgeshire throughout the year.

The Rural Group at County Hall are helpful in keeping the tracks and bridges in good repair, but a big benefit to the rider is that the level of population in much of the countryside is fairly low. Many tracks are not crowded with other riders or pedestrians, and it is then that one realises how enjoyable riding in Cambridgeshire can be.

CAMBRIDGESHIRE
ON HORSEBACK

LINCOLNSHIRE

(13) WISBECH

(14) PETERBOROUGH

NORFOLK

MARCH

NORTHAMPTONSHIRE

RAMSEY

CHATTERIS

(5) (3)

(9)

(4) (6)

(7)

ELY

(8) St. IVES

HUNTINGDON

(11)

(12)

SOHAM

KIMBOLTON

(1)

(10)

(18)

St. NEOTS

BEDFORDSHIRE

CAMBRIDGE

(19) (16) (17)

(2)

(15)

HERTFORDSHIRE

ESSEX

AN 11 MILE CIRCULAR TRAIL (ANTI-CLOCKWISE)

Ordnance Survey Maps:
Pathfinder: 982
Landranger: 154

Parking & Starting Point:
Parking is available in the National River Authority's grassy car park at Upware (GR.538700). You will find that this is well signposted and best approached by leaving the A1123 near Red Barn Farm (GR.552723) and travelling southwards along the unclassified road to Upware.

Of Interest:
This ride goes across the extremely flat countryside of the Fens. The black peat soil was once cut for fuel and is now prized for intensive agriculture. There are views of the villages along the higher chalk escarpment to the south, and, on clear days, of Ely Cathedral to the north east.

NB: At certain times of the year, such as harvest time in July and sugar beet harvest in December and January, there is a significant amount of heavy farm machinery using the single track fen roads. Most of these roads have wide verges and 'escape routes', but if your horse is really afraid of tractors avoid these times of year

Route Description:

Leave the car park and turn left past an old pumping station and go over a bridge. *Coming in from the left*

is Burwell Lode with its row of moored boats. Lode is the local name for rivers which have been straightened and banked. On the right is the River Cam. Take this opportunity to look at the views while you are up on the banks, before you descend to the level of the fen!

The many high banks around denote the rivers or Lodes as they are called in this part of the world. Waterways were very important for the facilities they offered communities in past times, and although Swaffham Bulbeck, which you will visit, had its Commercial End near the end of its Lode, and Burwell had a lot of waterfront activity, Reach (which you will also visit) seems to have been the most important place in this district and seagoing vessels of considerable size came up to it. One street in that village is called The Hythe; an old name indicating a port or jetty. It was the main port for Cambridge in the Middle Ages.

On the right, just as the road bends left down the bank, you can see Upware Washes, which are often flooded in winter and have been the site of fen skating competitions and are a great place for seeing wildfowl. Those of you who are bird watchers can spend a good few minutes spotting interesting birds. The footpath, which you pass, continues along the top of the river bank for 10 miles; all the way to Cambridge.

Continue down the metalled road onto the fen bearing left at

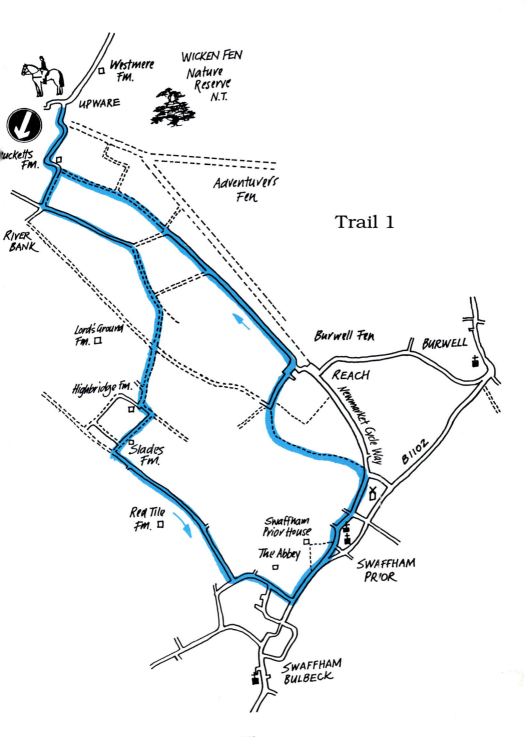

Westmere FM.

WICKEN FEN
Nature Reserve
N.T.

UPWARE

ucketts FM.

RIVER BANK

Adventurers Fen

Trail 1

Lord's Ground FM.

Burwell Fen

REACH

BURWELL

Highbridge FM.

Slades FM.

Newmarket Cycle Way

B1102

Red Tile FM.

Swaffham Prior House

The Abbey

SWAFFHAM PRIOR

SWAFFHAM BULBECK

Ducketts Farm (GR.535694) to the junction (GR.536693). Turn right here onto another metalled road and ride to the junction with a public telephone (GR.534688). Bear left here off the metalled road onto a peat track following a line of mature trees. *The track is a bit rough so take care until you pass the trees. In winter it can be very deep and boggy. As soon as you get past the trees the track is in perfect condition and offers a good place to canter if you wish. Continue for a mile to the end of the track.*

At the end of the track, at a barn, you join a tarmac road (GR.545682) and keep going in the same direction. *This road has a wide, even verge to the right.* After you have crossed a bridge (GR.547674) follow the road bearing to the right and eventually you will come to a crossroads (GR.546667).

At the crossroads, keep straight on. After about 500 yards there is a turning to the right, with a sign saying 'Greens of Soham, Lords Ground Farm Centre, leading to Commissioner's Farm' (GR. 544662). Ignore this turning and keep straight on. The road takes a bend to the left at Highbridge Farm (GR.544660) and, about 100 yards after you take the first right turn, up an unmarked concrete road (GR.545658). Ride straight up here until you meet the Swaffham Bulbeck Lode bank. Turn left. At first it is a bit uneven, but soon turns into a nice mile-long grassy track; an ideal place to canter if you wish, but please be considerate to other users. Eventually the track becomes stony again and you rise up to the bank top. Follow

this along until you come to Cow Bridge, a T-junction, with a farm on the left (GR.553635).

Turn left onto the metalled road, Fen Road. *The track you have just come down is marked public footpath, but it is in fact a byway all the way back up to the River Cam!*

The road you are following brings you into the older end of the village of Swaffham Bulbeck. *This is an area of the village called Commercial End dating back to the time before railways, when goods were brought by water along Swaffham Lode to The Hythe which, as at Reach, Burwell and Bottisham, gave importance to the place. One of the oldest houses, Abbey House, is on the left. This is a yellow and red brick house of 1778, the ground floor of which was the undercroft of the Nunnery of Swaffham Bulbeck which was founded in 1190. Other houses in Commercial End are old converted barns and warehouses and commercial buildings remaining from the village's past. Some have Dutch gable ends and other interesting architectural features.*

Follow the tarmac road straight on, ignoring the right turn into the village. Go up to a T-junction with the B1103 (GR.561632). Take care here as this is a busy, fast road. Turn left and follow this road for a short distance, turning left towards Swaffham Prior and Upware, past the gates of Swaffham Prior House and its deer park. Enter the village of Swaffham Prior (GR.565637).

Continue riding straight on along this road, all the way through the village until you come out the other side. Just past the last

house on the left, and before you come to a railway bridge, take a turning on the left signposted public byway 'Devil's Dyke Walks' (GR.572648).

Swaffham Prior is an interesting village, full of big old houses, and with a church yard containing two churches. The church furthest up the hill, St Cyriac's, is the younger of the two, and is owned by the Redundant Churches Fund. The other, St Mary's, has some early Norman work in the lower part of the tower - an octagonal base built long before the Ely Octagon was designed; this is the one used for services. The bells which are rung for service are in the redundant church, decorated in a Jacobean style. The two churches have had mixed fortunes suffering lightning strikes and other misfortunes. As one fell down, the other was rebuilt using stone from the other, until it was time for the first one to fall down. Other facilities in the village include a shop, public telephone and public house.

Continue down this byway which after about 200 yards turns into a nice grassy track.

On your right you will see a hill - Church Hill. Most of the top of this hill has been quarried out in the past for its stone; a local variety of chalk called clunch. Most of the older houses in the area, although they may look as if they are built out of brick, in fact have massive thick walls composed of clunch rubble, and the brick is only a facing. Clunch has been used as a building material since Roman times, for it was used in the basement of a Roman villa found near the Devil's Dyke. The delicate carving of the Lady Chapel at Ely Cathedral is made of clunch.

The track you are on is called Barston Drove, and was the old road from Swaffham Prior to Reach before the tarmac road was built. On the right you can see a low line of shrubs and trees. This is the Devil's Dyke, an Iron Age earthwork that stretches all the way to Woodditton, over 7 miles away. It is thought to have been an ancient defence stretching from the tangled woods of the east to the treacherous fens on the west, guarding the only open ground over which an enemy might advance, or cattle might be lifted.

This grassy track is perfectly safe if you wish to canter, until you reach the clump of trees on the left, keeping the hill on the right. It turns into stony track again and eventually joins a metalled road at a bridge with yellow railings and barns. Beyond is the white painted Spring Hall Farm (GR.561658). Turn right towards the village of Reach.

About 50 yards into the village, before you reach the village green, turn left over a bridge, signposted to Reach Fen. Then turn right along a track alongside the river, Reach Lode, on your right. For the next 50 yards, in wet weather, ride carefully along the edge of the track as it can be muddy.

It is worth a detour into this pretty and historic village, with its large green, and the tree-covered Devil's Dyke ending at the far end of the Green. This Bronze Age earthwork embankment stretches from Reach south eastwards for 7.5 miles to Woodditton, passing across Newmarket race course on the way. It has a Victorian church built 'with all the bold hideousness of which the

High Victorian decades were capable in their less genteel representatives.' (Pevsner, Buildings of England). There is a public telephone and a pub; all on the village green.

Continue along the track, which broadens out and has a good fairly grassy surface. It is worth noting that during a hot summer you may well find irrigators operating, especially up this stretch of track as a local farmer is involved in raising turf.

Half way up the track, past a stony stretch, a tarmac road joins the track at right angles from the left (GR.554677). Ride straight on. There is a good spot for a canter here if you wish. **Keep going until you** **approach a bridge which you cross. After this the track has a slightly uneven grassy surface with bushes on the left hand side and a huge ditch on the right side.** **Carry on along a tarmac road which joins in from the left, keeping in the same direction.** There is usually little traffic along this road. You will pass a little carrot washing factory on the right and you may find a tasty snack for your horse in the reject pile!

You will join the main tarmac road which comes in from the left (GR.537693) and follow it back to where you have parked your transport at Upware.

A 10 MILE LINEAR TRAIL

Ordnance Survey Maps:
Pathfinder: 1004, 1027 & 1028
Landranger: 154

Parking and Starting Point:
Parking is available on the wide grass verge at the western entrance to the village of Horseheath (GR.607473) reached from the A604. This area is on the right before the Old Red Lion Car Park. The A604 runs south-eastward from Cambridge to Haverhill and Colchester.

As this is a linear route alternative parking and pick-up points have been indicated on the map and are mentioned in the text. Parking at the finishing point (GR.493547) at the Gog-Magog Hills is restricted at the entrance and access is only suitable for vehicles less than 2 metres wide. However, there is a small pick-up point without this restriction.

Of Interest:
This linear trail offers 9.5 miles of off-road riding, crossing only two unclassified road and a B road throughout the whole of its length from Horseheath to near Cambridge. The green lanes of this route provide some of the best off-road riding in the country with ample provision for cantering should you wish.

There are no facilities on the route once you leave Horseheath, so it will be necessary to take refreshments with you. At Horseheath the 'Old Red Lion' public house serves meals and also has a large car park. There is a Post Office and telephone in the village.

Refreshments are served, just off the route, at Chilford Hall Vineyard (GR.567488).

This uncomplicated, but exciting, route follows part of the course of the Roman road from Colchester to Godmanchester near Huntingdon. It is not known what the Romans called this road, but in the Middle Ages it was called 'Wool Street' or 'Worsted Street'. In the 18th century antiquarians mistakenly thought it went to Chester (Deva) and called it the Via Devana and this name stuck.

The Via Devana was an early Roman road which was built just after the island of Britain was conquered by Claudius in AD 43, in order to link Colchester (Camulodunum) with the military area in the north. It is possible that it was built by the IX Legion, Hispana, who also built forts at Godmanchester and Cambridge. The trail, like the Roman road, does not pass through any villages, but goes straight across farmland and open countryside.

Route Description:

Leave your parking place and ride east into the village of Horseheath. Take the signposted

route to West Wickham which is near the village sign.

The well-made sign depicts two royal visits and that 'Plenipotentiary', who won the Derby in 1834, was bred and trained at Horseheath Lodge (GR.593476). The two crowns represent the visit in 1578 of Queen Elizabeth I and that in 1912 of King George V, who came to review his troops who were taking part in manoeuvres in the area. On the left is All Saints Church which has a medieval wooden screen. In the chancel

there are two large brasses and some interesting monuments. On the south side is a stained glass window recalling the Marshall family who have been prominent in the aircraft and motor industry in the 20th century and live in Horseheath parish.

Turn left onto the signposted public bridleway (GR.614477) which is the starting point of the Roman road - the Via Devana.

To each side, for the full distance of this trail, you will see large arable fields typical of the chalky uplands of Cambridgeshire. The crops grown are barley, wheat, beans, oilseed rape and peas. In summer, the edges of the trail have a profusion of wild flowers including both types of Scabious, Tufted Vetch and Greater Knapweed.

Ahead, to the left, distant views of the church-like water tower above Linton can be seen.

Just before Mark's Grave the trail descends to cross a small stream which is a tributary of the River Granta and gives an alternative name to the River Cam as it flows through Cambridge.

Ford the stream to reach an unclassified road (GR.595483). This is a suitable pick-up point with limited parking. **Cross the unclassified road and continue uphill on the signposted public byway.**

In Ad 60 the British tribes, under Queen Boudicca, rebelled against the

Map labels: NATURE RESERVE, Gog Magog Hills, Wandlebury COUNTRY PARK, A 1307, Hill Fms, Mag's Hill, Copley Hill, Lodge Fm., Meggs Hill, Worstead Lodge, A11(T), The Grange, Gunner's Hall, Roman Road, A 604

Romans and were gathering to sack St Albans (Verulamium) and the colony at Colchester (Camulodunum). At this time part of the Roman IX Legion, Hispana, was stationed at a fort at Longthorpe near Peterborough. It was from here that half the Legion set out with their commander, Petillius Cerialis in an attempt to save Camulodunum. As they were hurrying down this road they were ambushed and cut to pieces by the Boudiccan rebels and Cerialis was lucky to escape with his life. It is not known exactly where this event occurred, but it is not difficult to imagine them hurrying past you on this section of the Via Devana.

The trail joins the Icknield Way Path (GR.583487) and at this point it turns northwards to Balsham. You continue straight on. The Icknield Way Path, named after a prehistoric route that you will see later, is part of a published long dist- ance route. It includes a

riders route, which links the Ridgeway with the Peddars Way in Norfolk.

When you come to the B1052 (GR.574492) cross straight over. Do not follow the Icknield Way route along the road. This is another suitable pick-up point with parking.

Geologically this area is part of the great chalk ridge which runs from Salisbury Plain, through the Chiltern Hills into East Anglia and on into Norfolk as the Norfolk Edge. In the fields you will see flints which occur as hard nodules in the chalk. These flints are split giving a hard black face (knapped) and these are traditionally used to face buildings in this area. To the left is Chilford Hall which has vineyards and produces English wine.

Continue straight over at the unclassified road (GR.561498), between the posts and ride 2.4 miles to Worsted Lodge.

Trail 2

Roman roads were built in straight sections called 'alignments' and their surveyors changed the alignment according to the lie of the land. There was a small change of alignment (GR.561491) to enable the road to follow a reasonably level route.

On reaching the metalled road near Worsted Lodge (GR.529518) turn left and take the bridge over the A11 Trunk road. Please note that major changes made here in 1995 may not be as shown on your Ordnance Survey map. This is a suitable pick-up point with parking, only reached via the unclassified road off the A604 at Babraham (GR.516506). Just over the bridge continue straight but then bearing around to the right. At the T-junction, near Mount Farm, turn left back onto the byway and the Roman road.

At Worsted Lodge the Via Devana crosses the Romanised prehistoric Icknield Way, which is now followed at this point by the A11. *You will notice that there is a major re-alignment of the Romanised Icknield Way at this point.*

On this section of the trail there remains visible evidence of how the Romans built their roads. Ditches were dug each side of the alignment of the road and the surface of the road was raised one to three feet above the level of the surrounding landscape. This raised surface is called the 'agger'. Along this section the green lane is on a prominent agger 36 feet wide, 1-2 feet high.

You will see a signpost to a prehistoric circular ditch (GR. 505536) which is in Wandlebury Country Park (GR.495534). Continue riding for one mile to the end of the trail at the Gog-Magog Car Park (GR.493547).

After this point the Roman road follows the unclassified metalled road for a short distance and then realigns along the route of the prehistoric Worts' Causeway. Near Addenbrookes Hospital it re-aligns again and goes straight through Cambridge and out westwards as the A14 making towards the fort at Godmanchester. From here it joins Ermine Street and goes northwards to Lincoln (Lindum) and York (Eboracum).

NB: In writing this trail the author acknowledges his appreciation of the help given by the book 'In the Footsteps of Caesar: Walking Roman Roads in Britain' by Helen Livingston (1995) published by Ian Allan.

Roman Road

22

THE ELY TRAILS

The four Ely trails explore the area west and north west of the cathedral town of Ely. They cover an area of low fen 'islands' with villages and fenland typical of this area of Cambridgeshire, using an excellent network of public byways, bridleways and quiet unclassified roads. The trail commentaries will help you understand the life and land-scape of this unique area of Britain. Those who drive will notice the trails include the 16 mile Ely Riding and Driving Trail which is 73% off road. Visitors to the area should take the opportunity to visit the historic town of Ely with its cathedral, market and attractive river side walk.

Ely Cathedral

DOWNHAM AND THE FEN

TRAIL 3

A 14.5 MILE CIRCULAR TRAIL (CLOCKWISE)

Ordnance Survey Maps:
Pathfinder: 941
Landranger: 143

Parking & Starting Point: Parking is available on an area of ground (GR.526833) near Little Downham. This approached from Downham High Street (GR.523838) by turning down Chapel Lane with the clearly marked 'Baptist Sunday School 1930' on the corner. At the crossroads, go straight on, waymarked 'Public Byway' and 'Bishops Way'. The parking place is at the end of the metalled road on the wide grass area. This is also your starting point.

Of Interest:
This trail travels the fen to the west and east of the fen island village of Downham. On Ordnance Survey maps the village is called by its proper name 'Little Downham' to distinguish it from the larger Norfolk town of Downham Market - 13 miles further north; however it is known locally as Downham. The village is situated on a ridge of clay, sand and gravel, which is a northern extension of the 'isle' of Ely.

In earlier times the village was very isolated as it was virtually surrounded by marshy fen, but in the Middle Ages the Bishops of Ely built a 'hall' or palace' at Downham and it

became their favourite summer residence. Some remains and a reconstruction can be seen to the north of the village. The Bishops departed from Downham in 1710 and just after a start was made to drain the fens. This led to an increase in the amount of arable land farmed and a dramatic increase in the population of Downham, who were mainly employed in agriculture.

On this trail you will experience the vast skyscapes of the fens and see some of the original drainage channels of this artificial landscape. In some places you will be a metre below sea level and in others you will see the great banks and washes of the fen drainage channels. A dominant feature of the southern skyline will be the Norman Cathedral of Ely with its towers and 14th century central Octagon.

There are few facilities on the route and it is advisable to take food and drink along on your ride. In Downham there are two public houses and two general stores and you will also find a public telephone and post office.

If you are interested in birdwatching, then take along your binoculars and a recognition book to take advantage of an area rich in bird life.

NB: This trail can be quite easily shortened by referring to your map at Downham Hythe (GR.500839) or at the east end of Downham

(GR.521836), where alternative routes become obvious on the map.

Route Description:

Leave your parking place in a westerly direction and take the public byway called Clayway Lane, which is hedged on both sides and has a dyke on the right. *Downham can be seen on the ridge to the right.* **When you come to a gate (GR.523834), turn right and continue uphill on this narrow winding lane which bears left before reaching a metalled road (GR.521835). Turn left and follow this road taking a sharp right-hand bend (GR.522833). Continue along the road to turn right onto the public byway by West Fen Drove (GR.516833), keeping the concrete hard-standing on your left. At the footpath footbridge (GR.516834) follow the track left with a hedge to the left and a dyke on the right.**

When you come to the metal barn at Foxey Farm (GR.504832), turn right onto the metalled Redcaps Lane. At the T-junction (GR.503836) near Windyridge, turn left onto an unclassified metalled road and follow this road to the area known locally as Downham Hythe (GR.497837). *Hythe means a small port or jetty. It is difficult to imagine a port at Downham today, but in the middle ages, before the fens were drained, it was possible to travel to many places in the fens by water from the ports of the Wash.*

After a sharp right turn (GR.502835), drop down onto the fen along Downham Hythe Drove to Way Head (GR.487839). Turn right here along the road signposted Straight Drove. Bear left at the bungalow at the unusually named Three R's Farm (GR.487842) and continue towards the bank you can see in the distance. *These black fens are some of the best agricultural land in the country and traditionally grow potatoes, wheat, barley and sugar beet. You will, however, see some signs of livestock along this road. Pigs came onto the fen farms and smallholdings in the 1870's and were fed on surplus grain. A modern pig unit continues that tradition and sheep are sometimes seen grazing on sugar beet tops in the winter.*

At Bank House (GR.481855) turn right onto a newly-registered bridleway along the foot of the river bank. ***NB: DO NOT TAKE YOUR HORSE ONTO THE BANK; THE PATH ALONG THE TOP OF THE RIVER BANK IS ONLY A FOOTPATH.*** *If you wish to look at the Washes, get a friend to hold your horse.*

The view from the top of the bank is worth seeing. In front of you is the New Bedford River or Hundred Foot Drain and in the distance is the bank of the Old Bedford River. Between is the Royal Society for the Protection of Birds Reserve on the Hundred Foot Washes. In winter, when flooded, they are a haven for wildfowl and, in the summer, when dry, they also support a variety of plants, birds and insects. The banks and washes have traditionally been summer grazing for cattle and sheep.

The Duke of Bedford and other Adventurers put up money to build the Old Bedford River in 1631 and it was completed by the Dutch engineer

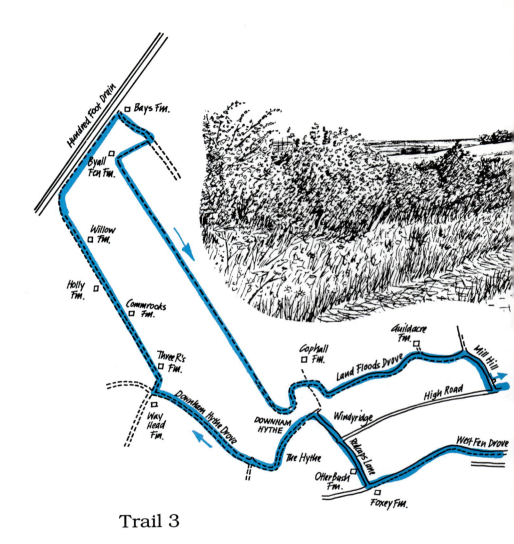

Hundred Foot Drain

Bays Fm.

Byall Fen Fm.

Willow Fm.

Holly Fm.

Commrooks Fm.

Three R's Fm.

Way Head Fm.

Downham Hythe Drove

DOWNHAM HYTHE

The Hythe

Otter Bush Fm.

Cophall Fm.

Windyridge

Foxey Fm.

Releurs Lane

Guildacre Fm.

Land Floods Drove

High Road

Mill Hill

Wet Fen Drove

Trail 3

26

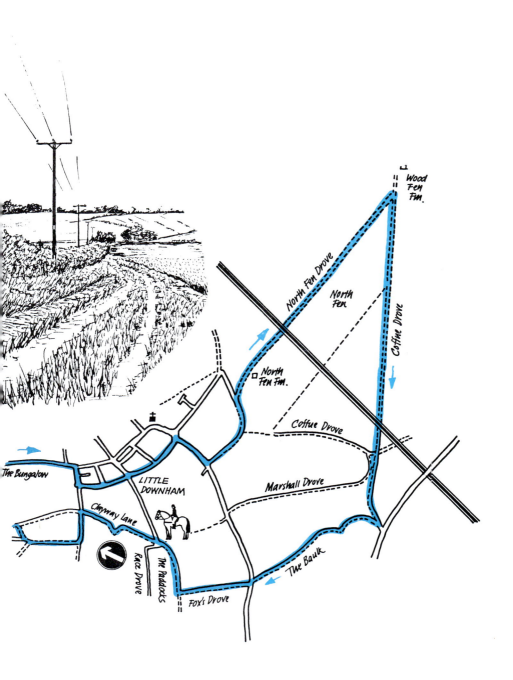

Wood Fen Fm.

North Fen Drove

North Fen

Coffue Drove

North Fen Fm.

Coffue Drove

LITTLE DOWNHAM

Marshall Drove

The Bungalow

Chewnay Lane

Race Drove

The Paddocks

Fox's Drove

The Baulk

27

Vermuden in 1637. The Civil War stopped the scheme and it was not until Cromwell took control that it was continued in 1651 when the New Bedford River was built and flood water storage in the Washes begun. The names Old and New Bedford River and Adventurers' Drove remind us of those times.

Continue riding on to the Oxlode Pumping Station (GR.483858). *Without this pumping station the fen as we see it today would not exist. Small drains move water from 2 metres below sea level into larger drains and eventually into the wide drainage channel of Oxlode. The electric automatic pumping engine lifts the water 15 or so feet into the New Bedford River from where it is taken down to Denver Sluice, into the River Great Ouse and finally flows into the sea at the Wash. All properties in the area contribute towards the cost of the drainage by paying an extra drainage rate on top of Council Tax.*

Continue on to the small settlement of Oxlode and turn right at the metal gates (GR.486863) onto the metalled Adventurers' Drove road. Turn right (GR.487860) along the rough track of Short Drove and ride to Byall Fen Farm.

The old farmhouse, built in 1887, shows some of the problems of building on peaty soil. The removal of water makes the peat shrink, which causes the foundations to show above soil level and this means that extra steps have to be built up to the front door. Uneven shrinkage has caused the house to tilt towards the main fireplace because the heat of the

fire dries out the peat even more This house has not been lived in fo over thirty years. To solve this ir modern times, bungalows are built or rafts of concrete and houses have t be supported by piles.

Turn left opposite the farm (GR.485858) and follow the Byal Drove in the direction of the electricity posts across Byall Fer for 1.50 miles. Ahead you will see Ely Cathedral showing above the Downham Ridge. When the Drove starts to curve to the left (GR.496837) it has a metalled surface. Follow this round and turn right (GR.499840). In a short distance, and near a bush, turn left (GR.499839) onto Land Flood Drove.

On reaching the metalled road (B1411) at Guildacre Farm (GR.508842), turn right. Take great care at this point as traffic appears quickly round the bend to the right. Use the verge. Continue along the B1411 around the right hand bend and up Mill Hill to the junction (GR.514838). Turn left, signposted Ely and Downham and continue towards Downham.

On the left across the field is Towe Farm, an antiques centre, where the remains of the Bishops of Ely's Palace can be seen. The village mair street is straight on and at its easterr end is the parish church of S Leonard. The church has an unusua Norman south doorway with twenty six carved faces 'of all sorts and sizes'.

After the village sign you come to a junction at the Plough Inn

(GR.519838). Turn immediately right, riding in front of the houses at 'Townsend'. On reaching the road, turn right riding downhill. *You will notice a standpipe with a flexible hose on the green to your left. This was used to fill up containers from the mains and is a remnant of the old village water supply. It is still used.*

On reaching 'Cannon Lane' (GR.521837), turn left into it and continue along this back lane which clings to the side of the slope. After passing a modern bus shelter on the right, you reach a crossroads (GR.528841). Cross the B1411 and turn right, signposted 'Ely' on the old signpost and 'Bishop's Way'. Ride on the wide verge between the trees and the field boundary. *Take care when crossing the busy Ely to Downham road.*

At the next junction (GR.531838) turn left into the wide Cowbridge Hall Road. Continue along the metalled road until you reach the junction with Beild Drove (GR.534842) where you keep left on the metalled road. After the sign 'Brick Kiln Road', on the left, turn right into the metalled North Fen (GR.533844). Here you drop down onto the fen. *You will notice that the soil is black. It was formed from decaying vegetable matter built-up over thousands of years by decomposing vegetation which grew in the marshy fens. When the fens were drained the peaty soils were exposed to the air and the soil shrank leaving the fields much lower than the road.*

When you come to the railway crossing STOP. It is an automatic level crossing and YOU MUST OBEY ALL THE INSTRUCTIONS. In the interests of safety it is suggested that you lead your horse over the crossing. The railway track links Ely and East Anglia with the Midlands via Peterborough.

At the house (GR.543857), the metalled road becomes a track and after the fourth electricity pole you leave North Fen Drove by turning almost back on yourself (GR.544861) to follow Coffue Drove southwards. *At this point on the trail you are one metre below sea level. Ahead in the distance you can see Ely and for almost two miles you will ride directly toward Ely Cathedral which lies on the horizon. Four prominent features dominate the skyline. In order left to right: the grain store and drier at Chettisham built in 1951; the water tower near the hospital; the Cathedral with its central stone octagon and higher west tower; and the spire of the parish church of St Mary.*

The track gradually leaves the fen (GR.544845) with the soil changing from black peat to brown clay. At the railway crossing (GR.544842) go through the tunnel to the right. *It is possible to go over the line using the gates, but it is safer to go through the tunnel. If you choose to cross the line then you MUST obey the instructions given to the letter i.e. you must telephone the signalman and open both gates before you cross. You must also dismount and lead your horse whichever option you choose.*

Shortly after the crossing keep left (GR.543839) up the bank continuing directly towards the Cathedral, with the dyke on the left. *To the right lie Chettisham Meadows (GR.540634); a specially managed haven for wildlife. To ensure that the many species of plants survive, the meadows are mown for hay and then grazed by cattle, avoiding the use of herbicides and fertilizers.*

Near the A10 (GR.543834), turn right under the electricity lines and continue right going over the brook away from the A10. Keep the brook to your left and continue along Balk Lane. *Balk is another spelling of baulk and in medieval times meant an unploughed area between the furrows in the medieval open fields. It became a pathway or boundary within these fields and this probably explains the name Balk Lane. The fields and their boundaries in this area are reckoned*

to be over 600 years old, dated by the fact that they have more plant species in them than younger hedges.

Bear right at the waymarker (GR.541834) and continue until you reach the B1411 (GR.534829). Turn left onto the metalled road (B1411) and then immediately sharp right following the sign 'Public Byway', into Fox Lane. *Care here as traffic approaches quickly around the bend to the left.* **Continue along this track to another waymarker (GR.528828). Turn right following the Bishops Way along Hurst Lane.** *You are now on a medieval track that the Bishops of Ely took from the Abbey at Ely to their Palace at Downham. The Palace was the centre of an estate that prospered in Downham for 500 years.*

In just over 0.25 miles you will come to your parking place and the starting point of your ride.

Byall Fen Farm

30

A 15 MILE CIRCULAR TRAIL (CLOCKWISE)

Ordnance Survey Maps:
Pathfinders: 941 & 961
Landranger: 143

NB: Much of this route is on newly upgraded bridleways and may not be as shown on your Ordnance Survey maps.

Parking & Starting Point:
Parking is available on the wide grass verges at the starting point known as Witcham Gravel (GR. 459823). To find this bridleway leave the A142 and follow the signs for Witcham. Go through the village of Witcham and continue until the road bends hard to the left (GR. 463804). At this point there is a turn right signposted to Wardy Hill. Go down this road, Hive Road, for just over one mile until it bends 90 degrees to the right. The bridleway goes off to the left from the middle of the bend.

Of Interest:
The highly fertile peat soils of the Fens are some of the most productive in the country. In the early part of the 17th century the Fens were drained by the 4th Earl of Bedford and a Dutch engineer, Cornelius Vermuyden, the resulting Ouse Washes providing habitat for many wild fowl. Riding through Coveney you will pass the delightful thatched Mansion Farm and the pretty 13th century Church of St Peter ad Vincula before turning left at the Victorian National School. Wild flowers grow in profusion around the fenland droves which were once used as a means of driving stock from the outlying farms to market. Ely Cathedral, 'The Ship of the Fens', can be seen from any point in the countryside.

Route Description:

From your starting point (GR.459823) follow the hard-core Witcham Gravel bridleway with its wide grass verge on the left. *(Note: this is a newly upgraded bridleway and may be shown as a footpath on your Ordnance Survey Map).* **On the right there are various allotment plots and a smallholding. At the end of this track there is a gate and a house on the right. Go through the gate (GR.456825).**

You are now at the base of the riverbank on a sanded track. The sand track was laid down in 1993 when the river bank was strengthened as part of the flood defence improvements. It was intended as a haul road for the heavy machinery used in the now completed work and can, therefore, become very hard in dry spells.

Turn right and go through a gate. Follow the river bank for about 1.50 miles. *The river bank has recently been upgraded to a bridleway and may still be* *signposted as a footpath. The track is fenced off from the river bank itself. The top of the bank is still a footpath and used for grazing cattle and sheep, you **MUST NOT** ride along the footpath. The Washes here are a haven for wild birds.*

Turn right (GR.470842) to leave the river bank by going through a gate onto Barbers Drove. *This has recently been upgraded to bridleway status and may still be shown as a footpath.* **You are now riding through arable farmland.**

At the T-junction (GR.473839) at the end of Barbers Drove, turn right onto a short drove and ride for about 0.25 miles until it turns left through 90 degrees and becomes wider.

Ride to the T-junction at the end of the drove (GR.472836) where you meet the Old Lynn Drove (Byway). Turn left and ride for about 1.25 miles. *This track can be muddy in wet weather.*

At the end of the Old Lynn Drove (GR.488839), having passed derelict houses, you will come out onto the road at Wayhead. Turn right and ride towards Coveney. *You will pass three farms all called Wayhead Farm!* **Ride along the wide grass verges alongside this road for about 1.5 miles until you reach the village of Coveney.** *You will pass Mansion Farm, a thatched, white building and the village church.*

In the middle of Coveney there is a left turn with a small traffic island in the middle. Turn left here (GR.489821). *This is called Green Drove and signposted to Ely, it*

passes the Old School and Lane Farm before leaving the village. **About 0.50 miles from the traffic island the road turns 90 degrees left, when you reach this point look for and take the Sedge Fen Drove which is on the right hand side at the centre of the bend (GR.495818).**

Sedge Fen Drove is a byway and starts off being tarmac but soon becomes dirt and then grass. **After a mile the track turns right and becomes Sweet Hill Drove** *(Sweet Hill is not a hill - it is flat!).* **You will pass some old farm machinery and then come to a small, tin shed on the left. Just after the shed is a left turn down a grassy track (GR.489811).**

Turn here. *This track is called New Drove and is a byway.* **Ride straight along it for 0.25 miles and turn left. Continue for a short distance to a T-junction where you turn right (GR.489805).** *The left hand track is private.*

Ride onto Old Fen Drove which goes uphill to turn left and then right before straightening again. At the end of Old Fen Drove you will come to a T-junction (GR.489797). Turn left onto Catchwater Drain and then almost at once turn right (GR.490797) onto Old Fen Baulk. This is a grassy byway going uphill. At the end of this track you ride downhill sharply and the track turns left and runs parallel with the Witchford Bypass.

This track - Grannys End Road - is fenced off from the bypass with posts and rails. In the spring it is planted

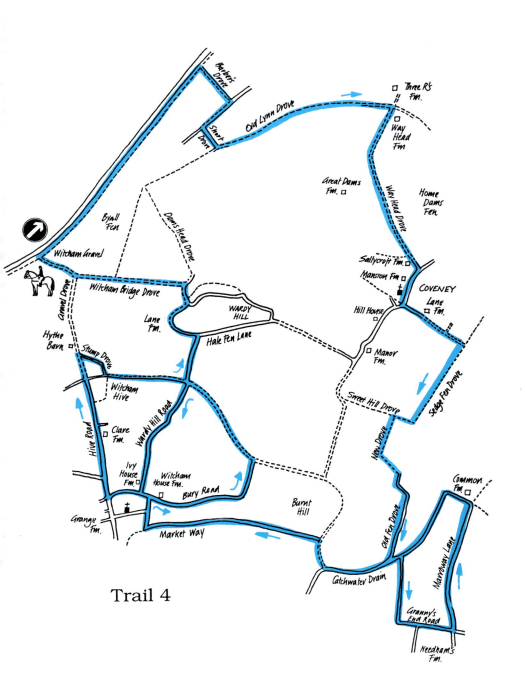

Barton's Drove

Three R's Fm.

Old Lynn Drove

Short Dam

Way Head Fm.

Great Dams Fm.

Way Head Drove

Home Dams Fen

Byall Fen

Dams Head Drove

Witcham Gravel

Sallycroft Fm.

Manston Fm.

COVENEY

Carmel Drove

Witcham Bridge Drove

Lane Fm.

WARDY HILL

Hale Fen Lane

Hill House

Lane Fm.

Hythe Barn

Stump Drove

Sweet Hill Drove

Sedge Fen Drove

Manor Fm.

Witcham Hive

Wardy Hill Road

Hive Road

Clare Fm.

New Drove

Ivy House Fm.

Witcham House Fm.

Bury Road

Burnt Hill

Common Fm.

Grange Fm.

Market Way

Catchwater Drain

Old Fen Drove

Marroway Lane

Granny's End Road

Needham's Fm.

Trail 4

33

with daffodils. *Please note that the Witchford Bypass may not be shown on your Ordnance Survey maps.* **At the end of Grannys End Road the track turns left onto Marroway Lane which is a grassy byway (GR.495790).**

Follow Marroway Lane for just over a mile until you come to a T-junction opposite Common Farm. Turn left (GR.494803) onto the Catchwater Drain which turns 90 degrees left after a short distance. Follow the Catchwater Drain for about 0.50 miles until you meet a road. Turn right (GR.483796) into Long Causeway and follow this as it winds round a shallow double bend, using the wide grass verges. After 0.25 miles you will see a track going left over a small brick bridge. Turn left here and go over the bridge (GR.483799).

This is a grassy byway known as Marketway. **Follow this byway for 1.50 miles until you come to the end of the track, passing two houses on the right and a farm yard straight ahead. Turn right onto the tarmac road (GR.466799). Ride up the road, going uphill, and into Witcham. Ignore the left turning into the village and pass Witcham House on the right.** *Witcham House is a large house with a ha-ha beside it; there are usually horses in the field.*

Ride straight on until you come to a T-junction where you turn right (GR.466803). The road here is very minor and the surface is well worn. Follow this road as it goes round Witcham House Farm on the right. *This is the home of the Holdervale family and their*

Hanovarian stallions. **Continue down the track as it becomes narrower and tree lined.** *This track is known as Bury Road and is a very attractive byway in the summer, however in winter the Witcham end can become very muddy.* **Continue to ride down the track for 1.25 miles until you meet the Catchwater Drain where you turn left (GR.476806).**

Follow the Catchwater Drain for a mile until you come to a crossroads of droves where you turn left (GR.470813) into the byway called Wardy Hill road. Ride along the track for about a mile, going uphill back into Witcham. At the top of the track you will pass Ivy House Farm before coming to a T-junction (GR.466803) where you turn down the drove going right. This grassy byway is known as Back Lane and goes through Witcham village coming out on the road in the middle (GR.463802).

Turn right here onto the road and follow the road to 'Hillcrest' which is a large house. Where the road bends left you will see a right turn on the bend, which appears to go straight on. Take this turn (GR.463804). This is Hive Road. *You will pass Clare Farm which is marked on the Pathfinder map as being on the right but is actually on the left hand side!. It is a single track road with good verges and very quiet.* **After about a mile the road goes over a small bridge with a big drainage ditch underneath. Ignore the signposted footpaths which lie to both sides just over the bridge and take the next signposted byway on the right known as**

Stump Drove (GR.460816).

Ride along this Drove until you meet the Catchwater Drain and turn left (GR.462813). This is a dirt byway with bushes on the left and a large ditch on the right. Follow it to the crossroads you came to earlier in the ride and this time turn left (GR.470813).

Ride along this byway going between hedges and passing fields containing sheep and cattle . After about 0.50 miles you will come to a crossroads of tracks where you turn left (GR.471817). This byway is Halefen Lane and comes out through the farmyard of Lane Farm. *As you pass Lane Farmhouse you will note that it is unusual in as much as it has a flat*

roof! **At the end of the track you are in the middle of Wardy Hill (GR.469821). Turn left.**

If you look to the right at this junction you will see the thatched Vineleigh Cottage which was restored in 1993 by English Heritage. Notice the unusual large, round chimney in the middle.

Ride on through the village using the wide grass verges, keeping the green and the houses and fields on the right. The road bends left and leaves the village. Continue riding along the lovely verges for about a mile and you will come to your starting point at Witcham Gravel (GR.459823).

Witcham

SAFETY

Know your Highway Code (1994 Edition)

In Particular Paragraphs 216/224

RIDE WITH:

CARE

- For the Land

COURTESY

- To other users

CONSIDERATION

- For the Farmer

DISCLAIMER

Whilst all due care was taken in the preparation of these maps neither the British Horse Society nor their agents or servants accept any responsibility for any inaccuracies which may occur. It should be borne in mind that landmarks and conditions change and it is assumed that the user has a Pathfinder or Landranger Ordnance Survey map and a compass.

The Country Code should be observed by every rider, with great care being taken to keep to the line of the Public Rights of Way Particularly when crossing farmland

A 14 MILE CIRCULAR TRAIL (ANTI-CLOCKWISE)

Ordnance Survey Maps:
Pathfinder:	941
Landranger:	143

Parking & Starting Point:
Parking is available on the northern verge of Witcham Bridge Drove (GR.463823) near the point where the public byway across Byall Fen reaches the metalled road. **DO NOT PARK IN A PASSING PLACE!** The best way to approach the parking area is to leave the A142 (GR. 463791) and take the unclassified road via the village of Witcham.

Of Interest:
Please note that there are no places on the route to purchase food so it is advisable to take your own with you.

Those interested in birdwatching should have binoculars and a recognition book to take advantage of an area rich in bird life.

This trail uses public byways and a long bridleway that follows below the great bank of the New Bedford River, or Hundred Foot River, for 4.50 miles. It can easily be shortened between Downham Hythe and Oxlode by taking Byall Fen Drove as shown on your Ordnance Survey map. The grade one agricultural land to the east grows wheat, potatoes, sugar beet, barley, oilseed rape and a fenland speciality - celery.

Route Description

Leave your parking place and ride northwards following the sign posted public byway across Byall Fen.

Before drainage took place in the 17th century, Byall Fen was a vast area and today the name occurs on both sides of the Bedford Rivers. Here the fen is 'black' and the peaty soil comes from decaying vegetable matter that collected over hundreds of years in the natural fen. Sometimes large tree trunks can be seen at the edge of the droves and these are known locally as 'bog oaks'. They grew in the fen over 6000 years ago when the climate was different and farmers find them in their fields when the plough strikes them beneath the surface. Sometimes you will see a newly ploughed field with small black 'posts' over it. These markers remind the farmers of the position of the bog oaks to be removed. They are difficult to saw through because of their soft, fibrous nature and on exposure to the air become very hard, so they have to be burnt.

Where a byway on the right from Wardy Hill meets the trail (GR.465832), continue riding straight on for 1.50 miles along 'Old Lynn Drove'. On reaching the metalled road at Way Head (GR.487839) continue across the green and ahead on to the metalled 'Downham Hythe Drove'.

After crossing the bridge over 'Grunty Fen Drain' (GR.495834), turn left on to a public byway. When 'Byall Fen Drove' enters from the left (GR.497837), you continue riding straight on, then go left and right until the next junction (GR.499840). Turn right and almost immediately turn left opposite a bush, onto the public byway 'Lands Flood Drove'. Continue along this winding track until you reach the metalled road (B1411) at Guildacre Farm (GR.508842). Turn left on to the B1411 and cross Westmoor Common. *Care - traffic approaches quickly from the right.*

A phenomenon that sometimes occurs in the spring in the black fens is a 'fen blow'. In order to sow seeds, a fine seed bed has to be prepared on these light soils. If this coincides with a period of strong winds, both soil and seed take to the air in great black clouds reducing visibility to nil. The fine dust penetrates everything, the seeds have to be re-sown and spring cleaning has to be done again!

Before reaching the Anglia Water compound (GR.498857), turn right onto the signposted public byway 'Firth Head Drove. *To the left is the fen hamlet of Pymoor, which spreads out in three directions along the straight fen roads. It seems to have trouble deciding how to spell its name; whether it should be 'Pymoor' or 'Pymore'. The maps give both spellings! Pymoor is part of Downham Parish and across the fen to the right, Little Downham Church can be seen at the eastern end of the ridge.*

After about a mile you pass the front of Dunkirk Farm (GR 515857) and then the drove bears to the left and reaches a metalled road (GR.517861). Turn left and follow the road through the small settlement of Dunkirk. At the bend (GR.514864), continue riding straight on to the wide signposted public byway - 'Furlong Drove'.

In this area you may see long mounds or 'clamps' at the corners of the fields. Inside these mounds are potatoes, which are stored through the winter under soil and straw in frost-free conditions until they are needed in the spring. Potato clamps are not so common nowadays because larger farms store their potatoes in buildings with automatic temperature control.

After one mile the trail reaches a metalled unclassified road (GR 508878), turn left and ride to the junction (GR.506877). Turn right signposted 'Wisbech 19 B1411 Welney 5'. At the sharp right-hand bend near Willow Kennels (GR 501882), turn left and follow the bridleway of orange shale at the foot of the Hundred Foot Bank.

For the next 4.50 miles the trail follows the Hundred Foot Bank and this is part of the six miles of newly registered bridleway added to the Cambridgeshire Definitive Map in 1995. For many years riders had ridden this path assuming it was a registered bridleway and were surprised when the National Rivers Authority put up gates and subsequently locked them.

Willow
Kennels

Railway Line

Sun Dell
Fm.

Home Fm.
House

Furlong Drove

Little Drove

Dunkirk
Br.

Dunkirk
Fm.

Pymore Lane

Frith Head Drove

Frith Head

PYMORE

Oxlode Fm.

Mount Pleasant
Fm.

Common
Bridge

Willow
Fm.

Guildacre
Fm.

Bays Fm.

Adventurers Drove

Westmoor
Common

Byall
Fen Fm.

Byall Fen Drove

Corhall Drove

Land Floods Drove

High Road

Straight Drove

Downham
Hythe

The Hythe

Downham Hythe Drove

Wayhead
Fm.

Barbers Drove

Old Lynn Drove

New Bedford River or Hundred Foot Drain

Byall
Fen

Witcham
Gravel

Witcham
Bridge Drove

Trail 5

39

One local rider, Rebecca Jackson, realised that over a long period of time public rights had been gained over the paths and set out to prove it. This meant she had to talk to people who could remember using the paths as of right, thinking they were part of the network of public rights of way. Eventually, with the help of the Cambridgeshire Rights of Way Department, she gained enough evidence to prove that rights existed and a route was developed as you see it today - thanks to Rebecca, who was willing to do something about it.

You have no rights, however, to take a horse to the top of the bank and ride the footpath that runs parallel to the bridleway. Please keep to the bridleway on the orange-surfaced haul road. If you want to look at the view from the top, someone must hold your horse whilst you take a look.

As you approach Oxlode Farm (GR.491870), look across the field and you will see a building with a rounded east end, looking like a church. This was the dual-purpose Pymoor and Oxlode School and Mission Church, built between the settlements to serve them both. This is now closed and is a private house. At the turn of the century, settlements near the river bank, like Oxlode, had higher populations and as you walk along this bridleway you will see evidence of sites where houses used to be.

Oxlode Pumping Station (GR.483858) needed workers living on site to work and maintain the steam and diesel engines especially if there was a flood alert. Nowadays there is an automatic electric pump, which is activated if water levels rise.

In a short distance (GR.479855), in the field to the left, is a concrete structure called a pill box, which was built around 1940 as part of the defence of England during the Second World War. A strong line of defence called the GHQ Line was put in place across the country to protect the manufacturing regions of the Midlands in case of possible invasion by Hitler. It went from Cambridge to Ely and then used the fen flood defences from here northwards. This pill box strong point and others along Adventurers' Drove (GR.496852) were part of this defensive line.

As you continue you will see ahead the village of Sutton and the church of St Andrew with its 14th century two-stage octagonal tower reminiscent of Ely Cathedral.

As the bank and the path bear to the right you reach Witham Gravel (GR.456824), and the end of the straight Hundred Foot Bank bridleway. Turn left on to a public byway - 'Witcham Bridge Drove'. There are often pigs at this point! **At the metalled road (GR.458824) bear left and return to your parking place.**

THE ELY DRIVING TRAIL

A 15 MILE CIRCULAR RIDING & DRIVING TRAIL (CLOCKWISE)

Ordnance Survey Maps:

Pathfinder: 941 & 961
Landranger: 143

Parking & Starting Point:

Parking is available on an area of grass near 'The Paddocks' (GR. 526833) close to Little Downham. This is approached from Little Downham High Street (GR.523838) by turning down Chapel Lane with the clearly marked 'Baptist Sunday School 1930' on the corner. At the crossroads go straight on, waymarked 'Public Byway' and 'Bishops Way'. The parking place is at the end of the metalled road on the wide grass area. Your route is described from this point.

Of Interest:

This route uses part of the other three trails in the Ely area to create a driving route using public byways and minor unclassified roads. A high percentage of the route is 'off road' (73%) and the unclassified roads are quiet. There are no gates and surfaces are generally good, but you should always take into account the time of the year and the weather conditions. Surface conditions may stop you taking the last part of the trail along Clayway Lane back to the starting point, but an alternative route on metalled, unclassified roads is given.

There are few facilities on the route and it is advisable to take your own food and drink with you on the drive/ride. In Little Downham there are two public houses serving food, two general stores and a public telephone and post office.

The landscape experienced includes the intensively farmed black fens broken by the fen ridge of Downham and the fen islands of Coveney and Witcham. The grade one agricultural land grows wheat, potatoes, sugar beet and barley.

Route Description:

Leave your parking place and follow the waymarked public byway, Hurst Lane, southwards keeping the drain on the left.

Here the trail follows 'the Bishop's Way', which at this point follows the route taken by Bishops of Ely to their summer palace at Downham-in-the-Isle. Before the fens were artificially drained, Downham was an island in the marshy, boggy fen and Hurst Lane was the driest route (probably only passable in summer) that they and their entourage could take to reach their palace with its pastures, orchards and vineyards. The Cathedral with its Octagon dominates the view southwards with the spired parish church of St Mary to its right.

At the junction with Fox Lane (GR.528828), continue straight onto the grass surface.

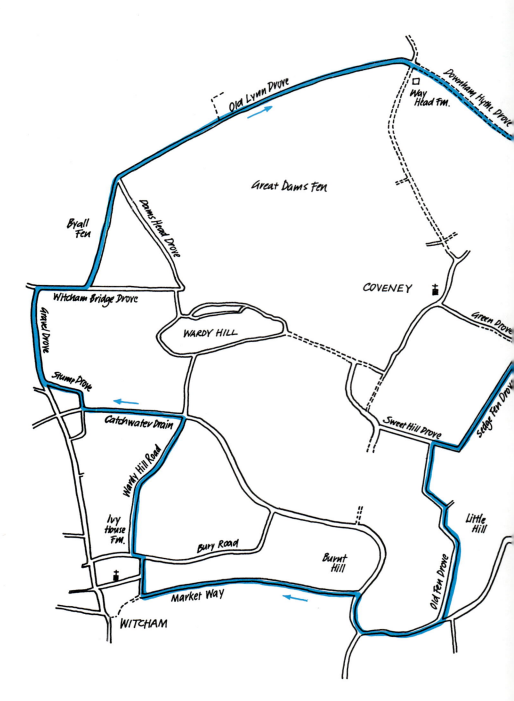

Old Lynn Drove

Downham Hythe Drove

Way Head Fm.

Great Dams Fen

Byall Fen

Dams Head Drove

COVENEY

Green Drove

Witcham Bridge Drove

Gravel Drove

WARDY HILL

Stump Drove

Catchwater Drain

Sweet Hill Drove

Sedge Fen Drove

Wardy Hill Road

Ivy House Fm.

Bury Road

Burnt Hill

Little Hill

Market Way

Old Fen Drove

WITCHAM

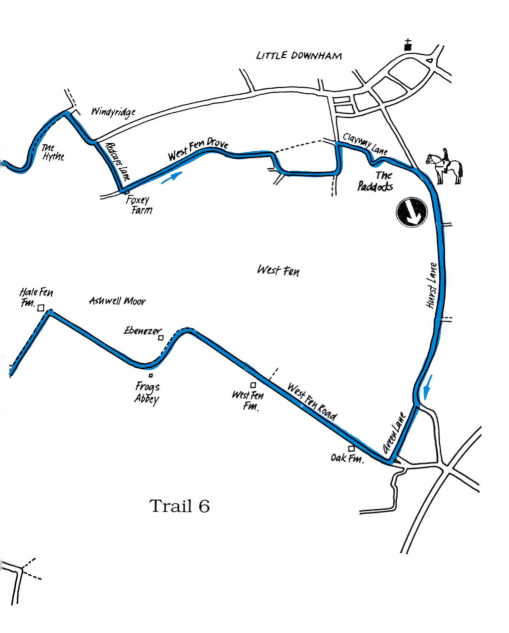

LITTLE DOWNHAM

Windyridge

The
Hythe

West Fen Drove

Clayway Lane

Redcars Lane

Foxey
Farm

The
Paddocks

Hurst Lane

West Fen

Hale Fen
Fm.

Ashwell Moor

Ebenezer

Frogs
Abbey

West Fen
Fm.

West Fen Road

Green Lane

Oak Fm.

Trail 6

43

Notice the uneven low fields to the right (GR.536823). You may wonder if the material excavated from this field was used to build the causeway across the fen.

At the railway sleeper bridge (GR.526816) continue straight on, but at the waymarked junction (GR.526814) turn right into the aptly named Green Lane.

Here you are at the edge of the 'isle' of Ely and at your nearest point on this drive to the Cathedral. To the right is the fen and to the left the smaller fields at the edge of the higher land.

At the metalled road (GR.524810) turn right and follow the bending, unclassified road to Coveney across the fen passing two farms with the name West Fen Farm, Ebenezer Farm, the newly built house at Frogs Abbey and Hale Fen Farm. At the next bend (GR.495818) continue straight onto the signposted public byway of Sedge Fen Drove. Just after taking the right hand bend (GR.491810), turn left at the corrugated building into New Drove (GR.488811). Continue until the T-junction (GR.489806) and then turn onto Old Fen Drove and continue to the T-junction with Catchwater Drain in front (GR.488796).

This is not the first time that you will come across the 'Catchwater Drain' and here it is a drain that 'catches' water coming from the 'highland' onto the fen.

Turn right on to the public byway following the Catchwater Drain to your left. At the metalled road by the bridge over the drain (GR.483796), turn right onto the unclassified road, Long Causeway. After travelling for 500 yards along this road around a left hand bend, turn left onto Market Way signposted 'Public Byway' and travel 1.1 miles to Witcham.

The width of Market Way indicated a droving road used to take animals to market in Ely.

After meeting the concrete road near Witcham (GR.466798), turn right onto the metalled Headley's Lane.

Witcham is a hill-top village typical of a fen island with the houses and farms clinging to the hill sides. Witcham is also the home of the World Pea Shooting Championships which are held in July!

At the road junction near Witcham House (GR.466801), continue straight on until just after Witcham House Farm (GR.466803) where you turn left, signposted public byway and after 150 yards turn right onto the wide public byway, Wardy Hill Road (GR.465803), which leads towards another hill top 'island' village, Wardy Hill.

On reaching the Catchwater Drain crossroads (GR.470814) turn left and follow the public byway, with the Drain on your left. At Witcham Hive (GR.463814) turn right onto Stump Drove. At the metalled road (GR.459816) turn right and follow Gravel Drove to the sharp

corner (GR.459824) and then bear right into Witcham Bridge Drove. After 525 yards turn left onto the signposted public byway (GR. 463823) to travel northwards across Byall Fen.

Here the fen is 'black' and this peaty soil comes from decaying vegetable matter that collected over hundreds of years in the natural fen. The soil is gradually decomposing and shrinking away and you will notice that the fields are lower than the byway, because the surface of the byway prevents the soil underneath from shrinking. The tree trunks, sometimes seen at the side of the track, are 'bog oaks'; trees that grew 6000 years ago and have been preserved in the peaty soil. The constant shrinkage brings them to the surface. Farmers find it difficult to saw them up, so they are left in piles and burnt.

Where the byway on the right from Wardy Hill meets the trail (GR.465832), continue travelling straight for 1.5 miles along 'Old Lynn Drove'. On reaching the metalled road at Way Head (GR.487839) continue round the green and onto the metalled 'Downham Hythe Drove'. Cross the Grunty Fen Drain (GR.495834) and climb the ridge up to the left hand bend (GR.496834). Turn left with the metalled road, going through the hamlet of Downham Hythe, following the road until you reach the junction (GR. 500838). Here turn right towards Windy Ridge and at the bend (GR.503836) turn right into Redcaps Lane.

At Foxey Farm (GR.504832) turn left on to the public byway - West Fen Drove and drive to the point where a footpath enters onto the byway over a footbridge (GR. 516834). Bear right with the byway until you reach a metalled road (GR.516833). Continue along this road around the left hand bend until you reach the junction with Clayway Lane (GR.521835)*. Turn right here and follow this winding public byway to your parking place (GR.526833).

* At certain times of the year, Clayway Lane, as its name suggests, can be very wet from the water draining down the slope from the Little Downham ridge. An alternative, drier route, along metalled roads can be taken by going straight on at the Clayway Lane junction to the junction with Cannon Street (GR.521837). Turn right here and go to the crossroads (GR.524837). Turn right passing the island and return to your parking place (GR.526833).

UPTON, STEEPLE & LITTLE GIDDING

TRAIL 7

A 12 MILE CIRCULAR TRAIL (CLOCKWISE)

Ordnance Survey Maps:
Landranger: 142
Pathfinder: 939 & 959

NB: *Due to the heavy clay soil in this area, some of the tracks could need care in wet weather.*

Parking & Starting Points:
Parking is available at Christ's College Farm, Upton (GR.174785) by kind permission of the farmer. It is essential to telephone in advance on 01480 891059 to book a parking place as the yard is rather small. Upton lies 0.50 miles off the A1 (northbound). If travelling south on the A1 take the turn off for Alconbury, signposted B1090 and follow the signs for Alconbury Weston. Turn right in the village and this road takes you to Upton. In Upton go left by the church and the farm is on the left.

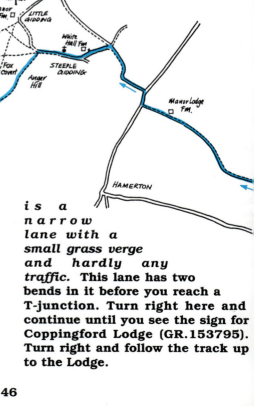

Route Description:

On leaving Christ's College Farm, turn left to join the bridleway. Ride straight along this track passing a Christmas Tree plantation on the left. *You might see bullrushes in the ditch on the right.* **When you reach the metalled road, turn left (GR.165800). This** *is a narrow lane with a small grass verge and hardly any traffic.* **This lane has two bends in it before you reach a T-junction. Turn right here and continue until you see the sign for Coppingford Lodge (GR.153795). Turn right and follow the track up to the Lodge.**

Coppingford village no longer exists and even the banks and ditches that marked the sites of the medieval houses have been destroyed. The original main street, an unusually wide hollow, can still be seen.

Ride to the right between the barns and join the well defined track to Manor Lodge Farm. Go through the farm yard and join the farm drive which takes you down to the road. Turn right here and ride along the grass verge and then take the next turn left signposted 'The Giddings' (GR.140810).

At one time, the Giddings, Great, Steeple, and Little, were of a similar size. In the 16th century it seems likely that Steeple and Little Gidding were put down to mostly grass and this significantly reduced the population these two villages could support. Great Gidding, however, retained the open strip method of farming until very much later, some until 1869. This meant that this village could support a much greater population and so has remained a much larger community than the other two. The name Gidding comes from 'Gydela's People' and the suffix 'Gredat' was added to the northernmost village by 1252. Great and Little Gidding were assessed as one for the domesday Book but Steeple Gidding was assessed separately. This was probably because in pre-Conquest documents, Steeple Gidding belonged to the Abbot of Ramsey.

At the telephone box, turn left and follow the lane past Steeple Gidding Church and here the bridleway begins again. Sometimes the gate across the track is locked, but there is plenty of room to ride around the left hand post. **From the bridleway sign, ride down the track to the second hedge, which also has a bridleway sign. Turn left and follow the track down the hill and turn left at the sign for The Giddings, and then turn right at the corner of the field and continue riding down the hill. At the bottom follow the signpost straight on but**

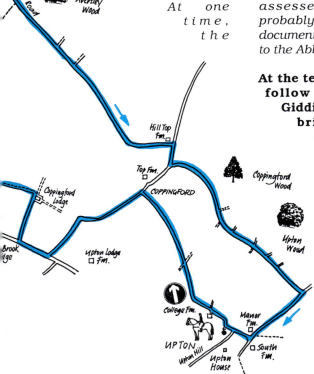

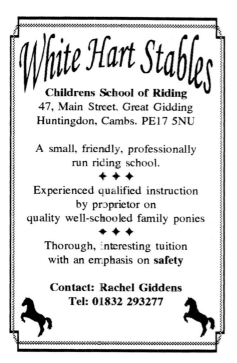
to the right of the hedge. At the bottom of the hedge turn right following the waymarker (GR.125808). There is a stream on your left and you keep on this straight path. There are two bridges over the stream with concrete run-ups. You will have to ride over this concrete but DO NOT CROSS THE BRIDGES. There is also a waymarked track to the right. Do NOT take this track but keep the stream on your left until you reach the hedge (GR.120818).

Here go through the hedge, over a small ditch; which is really just a dip in the ground! Immediately turn right and ride up the hill. You will ride through three fields as you go up the hill going through two gates. *DO NOT JUMP the cross country fences next to the gates. Beware of the bank*

under the hedge on you right as you go up the hill as it is, in places, covered with rabbit holes. The third field can get very wet and boggy near the hedge in winter so you may have to ride on the edge of the track.

When you reach the road, go through the gate and turn right. A short distance down this road there is a track to the left which is waymarked. (GR.129824). Turn left onto this track. *Sometimes the gate across the entrance to this track is locked but you can ride around the left hand post taking care to avoid the ditch on the left.* Keep along this track passing a wood on your right. Continue until you reach the ditch, which sometimes has a stream running along it, where you turn left (GR.138832). Follow this well defined track with a wood on your left and the ditch on your right until the bridleway bears left away from the ditch and then right following the fence until you reach a bridge over the ditch. Cross the bridge and ride alongside the ditch, which is now on your left, until the footpath continues ahead and the bridleway turns right up the hill. Keep on the bridleway until you reach the second gate when you turn right onto the Bullock Road (GR.140840).

Bullock Road is a 25 feet wide track and a former cattle drovers route. Follow this historic route for about 3 miles as it runs parallel with the A1. Just before Cold Harbour Farm (GR.145830), there is a short section of metalled road which is only single track, but has good wide verges. **Join the drovers route again and continue straight on**. *There are good views to Hammerton to the west.* **Continue on with Aversley Wood on the left.** *Look out for toads in the breeding season as they use this route when returning to their breeding ponds. On the right you can see the remains of Coppingford Church and Manor House in the fields.* **When you reach Hill Top Farm, turn right onto a short stretch of road then turn left to rejoin Bullock Road (GR.169804).** A short distance on you pass a radio mast. The track turns left just past the mast but the Bullock Road carries straight on. You will pass first Coppingford Wood and then Upton wood both on your left. Keep to the wood side of the track. Just after Upton Wood you reach the road and turn right here remembering to shut the gate (GR.182789). *The road is narrow and quiet but does go up to the A1. There is a single verge.* Follow the road into Upton and track right past St Margaret's Church by the village pond. This takes you back to Christ's College Farm.

Upton Church

49

ACROSS THE ALCONBURY BROOK VALLEY

TRAIL 8

A 14 MILE CIRCULAR TRAIL (ANTI-CLOCKWISE)

Ordnance Survey Maps:
Pathfinder: 959 and 939
Landranger: 142

Parking and Starting Point:
Parking is available on the wide grass verge (GR.139807) near Hamerton. This is also your starting point.

NB: A shorter trail of 10 miles can be ridden by following the directions in the route description.

Of Interest:
This trail crosses and re-crosses the valley of the Alconbury Brook, a tributary of the Great Ouse, and explores the Huntingdonshire Heights on either side which reach a height of 200 feet. Agriculturally it is arable country on heavy clay soils; growing wheat, barley, sugar beet and oilseed rape, with few livestock to be seen.

It is important to take your own food and drink as there are no public houses on the route and no places where food can be purchased at all times of the year. During the summer season, there is a chance of light refreshments at the Hamerton Wildlife Centre between 10.00am to 6.00pm. Public telephones are available at Hamerton, Barham, Buckworth and Upton.

Route Description:

From your parking place ride down the hill towards the village of Hamerton passing the Hamerton Wildlife Centre entrance on your left. At the road junction turn right, signposted 'Winwick 2, Leighton Bromswold 3' and ride over the Alconbury Brook for the first time.

Up until the 1960's there was a ford at this point and the only 'dry' way across was the small white bridge seen across the field to the left. Hamerton is in two parts which are divided by the brook, with the church of All Saints, the old rectory and the old school and farmhouse on the higher west bank and the rest of the village on the east bank.

At the next road junction bear right, signposted 'Winwick 2'. *Ahead you will see the steeple of Winwick Church.* **After approximately 0.75 miles turn left onto a signposted bridleway with a grass and granite chip surface (GR.123799). Hamerton Grove Nature Reserve is on your right but there is no public entry on this bridleway.**

Pass around a metal gate (GR.119794) and ride straight on to a partly metalled road for 100 yards, bear right to go through the hedge and immediately turn left onto a grass track. Just after

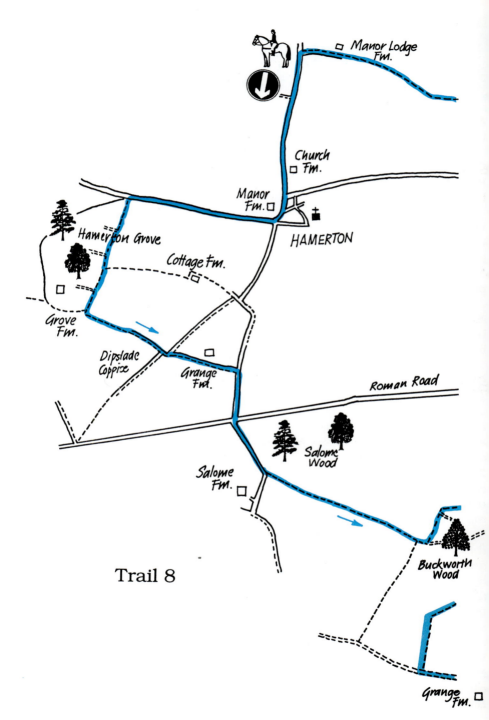

Manor Lodge Fm.

Church Fm.

Manor Fm.

HAMERTON

Hamerton Grove

Cottage Fm.

Grove Fm.

Dipslade Coppice

Grange Fm.

Roman Road

Salome Wood

Salome Fm.

Buckworth Wood

Grange Fm.

Trail 8

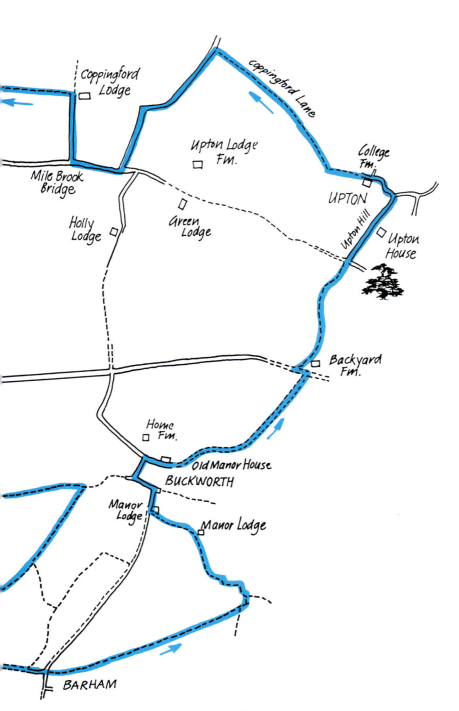

Coppingford
Lodge

Coppingford Lane

Upton Lodge
Fm.

College
Fm.

Mile Brook
Bridge

UPTON

Holly
Lodge

Green
Lodge

Upton Hill

Upton
House

Backyard
Fm.

Home
Fm.

Old Manor House
BUCKWORTH

Manor
Lodge

Manor Lodge

BARHAM

53

passing near a field boundary on your right (GR.118796), turn left. Follow the grass bridleway passing between a hedge on the left and a young plantation. Continue riding until you reach a hedge, turn right here and then go left through the hedge in the corner of the wood (GR.119788). Ride to the end of the wood and turn right through a gap in the hedge. Immediately turn left continuing to ride downhill to Grange Farm. At the bottom of the slope ride straight on following the hedge to the left and go between the grey barn on the right and Grange Farm. Continue straight on keeping the hedge to your left until you reach the metalled road. Turn right at the bridleway sign and continue to the T-junction (GR.125779).

Here the route crosses the line of a Roman road running between Ermine Street (London to York) at Alconbury and Ratae (Leicester). For much of its route in this area it is still used as a road today.

Take care here as traffic can be fast along this straight stretch of road.
Turn right signposted 'Old Weston 2, Oundle 10' and then immediately turn left signposted 'Leighton Bromswold 2, Spaldwick 4'. Continue riding ahead going through Salome Wood until you reach the bend in the road just before Salome Lodge Farm with it's tall silo, where you turn left at the bridleway sign (GR.126775).

Aim towards the right hand edge of the wood which lies across this large arable field , and at the foot of the slope cross over the stream and make for the nearest hedge boundary still keeping the wood ahead of you (GR.134768). Keeping the hedge on your right, ride for approximately 100 yards to the corner, go through the hedge to the right and continue uphill keeping the hedge to your left.

At the waymarker at the corner of Buckworth Wood turn left keeping the wood to your right. On reaching the next waymarker at the end of the wood, turn right and cross the field towards the village of Buckworth keeping the small copse and pond on your left. After riding between a derelict farm building on the right and 5 storage silos on the left, go straight and then turn right at the waymarker post (GR.144767) onto a grass track.

If you wish to take the shorter 10 mile route continue straight on the bridleway to Buckworth village. On meeting the metalled road, turn left into Church Street and re-join the longer route. *(GR.148767)

After 250 yards cross over the drainage ditch at the waymarker post and continue to follow the track keeping the drainage ditch on your left until you reach a metalled road (GR.132758).

Ahead across the valley to the west can be seen the village of Leighton Bromswold and its fine church with a tower. You have reached a height of around 200 feet, which is the general level of these Huntingdonshire hills.

Turn left and continue riding along the metalled road towards the village of Barham. At the T-junction (GR.137755), turn left signposted 'Buckworth 1 1/2'.

To the right is the hamlet of Barham and on the corner is the small church of St. Giles. Inside it has box pews and 17th century benches.

Ride for about 50 yards then turn right onto a rutted bridleway, keeping the hedge on your left and continue to the end of the hedge (GR.143754). Do not follow the rutted path which takes you towards the derelict buildings at Lodge Farm. Instead bear slightly left and cross the large field by descending to the stream and then making uphill towards the hedge and line of trees. The bridleway goes into the corner (GR.149754).

Go through the gap in the hedge and follow the track towards the dead tree to the right of the electricity pylon. On reaching the dead tree there is another bridleway coming in from the right and a concrete road from the left (GR.153755). Turn left onto the concrete road and follow it towards the farm buildings at Manor Lodge. *You can see Buckworth Church spire behind them.*

Turn left in front of the buildings (GR.151762), and follow the track around them towards the second Manor Lodge. Ride on until you reach the metalled road with a bridleway sign (GR.148764), then turn right and go into the village of Buckworth going round a left hand bend, turn right at the next junction and ride into Church Road (GR.148767).

The shorter route re-joins here. Buckworth is a small village, but surprisingly has a cricket club that has its clubhouse opposite the church. The Church of All Saints has a notable late 13th century steeple, which can be seen for most of this trail. The church has a number of grotesque gargoyles and high up on the west side of the steeple is a carved green man with foliage coming out of his mouth.

At the T-junction at the end of Church Road, turn right onto the metalled road signposted 'Alconbury Weston 2' and follow this road for just over one mile to Brickyard Farm (GR.163771). On reaching another T-junction take the signposted bridleway opposite. Ride through the side gate to the right of the metal gate and follow the chain link fence across the grass field to the next gate, then follow the route along the field boundary. On reaching the corner turn right around the copse. After about 50 yards go on to the left through the hedge and down to the bridge over the Alconbury Brook (GR.165776).

The Alconbury Brook is a tributary of the River Great Ouse and it rises about 12 miles to the north near the Northamptonshire border and flows into the Great Ouse near Huntingdon.

Cross the bridge with its high side rails and then ride parallel to the brook for a short way to turn right, and follow the track towards Upton keeping the drainage ditch on your left. Continue riding straight on until you reach the metalled road signposted 'Upton 1/2'. A steepish climb then takes you into the village of Upton.

Upton is on the east side of the valley and its small church of St Margaret has a spire that competes with that at Buckworth. The village sign is adjacent to an attractive duck pond.

Just after passing the church, turn left into Green Lane, and on reaching the end of the houses on the left, go from the metalled road onto the green Coppingford Lane which is signposted 'Coppingford 1'.

You are now riding along an old medieval route that developed after the A1 route of Ermine Street was abandoned at the end of Roman times. Travellers left Ermine Street further south and passed along the main street of Upton to Coppingford and beyond eventually to cross the River Nene at Wansford. As you ride along this 'high' lane at about a height of 50 metres, look to the right and notice the distant view across the Cambridgeshire Fens. To the left there are views across the Alconbury Brook Valley to Buckworth.

Continue riding along this green way until you reach a part of the route with high hedges on each side and eventually the metalled road at Lodge Farm, Coppingford (GR.165799).
Coppingford no longer exists and the banks and ditches that marked the site of this medieval settlement have been destroyed. Beyond Coppingford old footpaths, green lanes and unclassified roads mark the route of the medieval routeway for another 8 miles.

Ride on and turn left on to the metalled road. Follow this road around a sharp right hand bend and then a left hand bend and continue until you reach a T-junction (GR.155793). Turn right here and continue on the metalled road signposted 'Hamerton 1 1/4, Winwick 3 1/2', until you reach Mile Brook Bridge (GR.153794). Turn right. At the bridleway sign ride onto the concrete road to Coppingford Lodge. At the farm ride straight between the farm buildings and after the last building on the left (GR.154799), turn left and go over the stream and follow the track parallel to the electricity lines.

Take the well defined route to Manor Lodge Farm. Turn onto the metalled road here and follow it until you reach the unclassified metalled road (GR.139808). Turn left and your parking place is immediately to your right.

Buckworth Church

THE BRITISH HORSE SOCIETY

BHS BOOK AND GIFT SHOP

The largest specialist Equestrian Bookshop in the UK displaying a comprehensive range of equestrian books and videos

The British Horse Society Book and Gift Shop is situated at the British Equestrian Centre on the Showground at Stoneleigh (on the B4113), and is open Monday to Saturday 9am-5pm. A Full mail order service is available. Phone now for free catalogues.

Tel: 01203 690679

BHS Book and Gift Shop
Stoneleigh Park, Kenilworth
Warwickshire CV8 2LR

Registered Charity No 210504

The British Horse Society

A 10 MILE CIRCULAR TRAIL (CLOCKWISE)

NB: This trail links in with Route 21, Barnwell, in Northamptonshire on Horseback.

Ordnance Survey Maps:
Pathfinder: 939
Landranger: 142

Parking & Starting Point:
Parking is available on the highway in Thurning, near the telephone kiosk (GR.087832). It is best approached by leaving the B662 at Clopton (GR.064803) and travelling north east towards Thurning. On reaching the church on your right (GR.086828), continue straight across. At the next junction (GR.086830) go straight on between the houses and you will see the telephone kiosk on your left. This is your starting point.

Of Interest:
This trail is mainly in Northamptonshire and only crosses into Cambridgeshire for a short distance, near Great Gidding, but for nearly two miles it follows an old route that marks the boundary between the two counties. This ride also links with a route starting at Barnwell (GR.051848), which is Route 21 in a companion volume - 'Northamptonshire on Horseback'. Linking the two routes in a clockwise direction, gives a total distance of 18.5 miles. Further details can be found on the map and in the route description.

The parish of Thurning has had a strange administrative history: being at one time partly in Northamptonshire and partly in the old county of Huntingdonshire. From 1889 it has been wholly in Northamptonshire, but archive material is found in the record offices of both counties.

The rocks are mainly clay with the glacial boulder clays on the higher ground and the Oxford clay exposed in the valley of the Alconbury Brook. Agriculture is mostly arable with some very large fields growing wheat, barley and oilseed rape.

There are no facilities on this ride, so it is advisable to take your own food and drink. In Great Gidding (GR.117830), just off the trail, there is a post office/general stores and a public house.

Route Description:

Keeping the telephone kiosk to your left, ride to the corner and turn left into the metalled 'No Through Road', which is a few yards from your parking place. After 100 yards keep right and take the waymarked bridleway signposted - 'Hemington'. Bear right (GR.087833) across the grass field through the jumps of the Cromwell Equestrian Centre, making downhill towards the

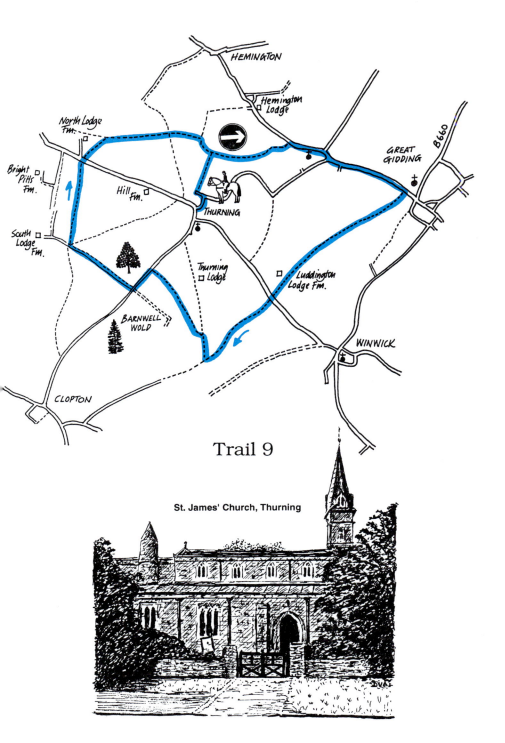

HEMINGTON

Hemington Lodge

North Lodge Fm.

Bright Pitts Fm.

Hill Fm.

THURNING

South Lodge Fm.

Thurning Lodge

Luddington Lodge Fm.

BARNWELL WOLD

CLOPTON

GREAT GIDDING

B660

WINWICK

Trail 9

St. James' Church, Thurning

bridlegate. Follow the grass to the hedge (GR.089838) and turn right. *Do not follow the circular route.*

On your left is a stream which is the infant Alconbury Brook. It rises near here and flows south for 12 miles to enter the River Great Ouse near Huntingdon.

At the end of the hedge on your left, cross over the bridge with the bridlegate (GR.095837) and continue keeping the brook to your left. At the concrete bridge (GR.100838) turn left over the brook and ride to the road.

Turn right (GR.101838) onto the metalled road. *You are now entering the small, shrunken village of Luddington in the Brook, which is notable for its almost complete change of location and layout in the 19th century. To the right, in the wood called 'Great Hall Spinney' (GR.102837), there are earthworks which are thought to be the site of the Manor House. Next you will see the isolated church of St Lawrence, which indicates the original position of the village straddling the Alconbury Brook. Hence the name - Luddington in the Brook!*

By the mid 19th century most of the houses had gone from this position and, what houses there are today, are sited along the 'new' Hemington-Great Gidding road built at the time of the enclosures in 1808. This is the road that you are riding along.

At the junction (GR.106836) continue straight on, signposted 'Great Gidding'.

Soon you will ride over the unmarked county boundary into Cambridgeshire

and ahead you will see the spire of St Michael's Church, Great Gidding.

Just after the 'Great Gidding' sign, turn right onto the signposted public bridleway (GR.115832). *The uneven, sometimes muddy, surface here indicates the exposed Oxford clay in the valley. Re-cross the Alconbury Brook by the bridge and follow the bridleway sign indicating the route to the right of the hedge.*

Now you start riding an old route between Great Gidding and Clopton which follows the Northamptonshire /Old Huntingdonshire border for nearly two miles; the bridleway being on the Northamptonshire side. On the other side of the boundary hedge, in Cambridgeshire, you can see the 'Hunt Ride'. This is a private ride, owned by Milton Estates, and it is used by the training stables in Great Gidding. The village has a number of horse-related businesses and this interest is thought to have started when the Fitzwilliam Hunt moved their kennels from Milton, near Peterborough, to Great Gidding for the duration of the Second World War.

Continue on the bridleway as it climbs and go through a hedge (GR.102822) where the surface levels are around 200 feet. Ride to Luddington Lodge Farm (GR.099820) where the bridleway changes to a metalled surface. On reaching the metalled highway (GR.096816), cross straight over onto the wide, signposted public byway.

On your left you will see the village of Winwick. The byway is most attractive and in the spring there are cowslips and violets. Here you can experience travelling along a road as it was before the invention of metalled surfaces and the motor car.

Turn right (GR.086807) and follow another wide lane which looks like a byway, but is a bridleway. *In the 18th century a gibbet stood here at this isolated meeting point of parishes and counties. The continuation of the lane to Clopton is called 'Gibbet Lane'.* **When the wide lane ends (GR.086811) the trail goes through a bridlegate and around the left of the field. Go through the hedge (GR.084815) and follow the edge of the wood keeping the hedge on your left and crossing the bridge (GR.083818). At the metalled road (GR.079822) turn left at the sign and ride along the road until you turn right at the public bridleway sign (GR.076818) and follow the well defined track. On reaching an old oil tank marked 'CHARRINGTONS' near South Lodge (GR.068826), turn right and keep the wood on your left.**

It is at this point that the trail links with Route 21, 'Barnwell' in Northamptonshire on Horseback, and if you are following the linked route you should turn left here.

The surface changes from granite chippings to grass (GR.069829). Here the trail reaches its highest point of nearly 250 feet and to the right can be seen the small spire of Thurning Church and on the left the Nene Valley.

On reaching the metalled highway (GR.071838), cross over and follow the signposted bridleway across the field. At the hedge (GR. 074841) cross over the brook and follow the bridleway keeping the hedge to the right.

It is here that Route 21, Barnwell, Northamptonshire on Horseback, rejoins this linked route.

You will see a water tower to your left. Go through the bridlegate (GR.079841) into a grass field, still keeping the hedge to your right.

Here there is a change in the landscape with the next few fields left as pasture. This has allowed cultivation remains of the medieval common fields of Thurning to survive. The ridge and furrow of the medieval strips are very clear and you can even see how a curve developed at the headlands, near the brook, where the oxen curved round in order to turn. The parish of Thurning was not enclosed until 1839, when the Enclosure Commissioners Surveyors laid out the fields in this area with the quickthorn hedges we see today.

At the corner of the grass field (GR.084841), turn right through the gate and then immediately left into the next grass field following the hedge which is now on your left. Leave this field by the bridlegate (GR.086841). Continue until you reach a bridge (GR.087840) where a public bridleway and a brook enter from the left. Here continue right following the stream. Turn right (GR.089838) and retrace your route back in the opposite direction to the field with the jumps. Turn left (GR.087833) onto the metalled road and into Thurning. At the junction turn right and you will see your parking place.

A 16 MILE CIRCULAR TRAIL (ANTI-CLOCKWISE)

Ordnance Survey Maps:

Pathfinder: 980
Landranger: 153

Parking & Starting Point:

Parking is available at the Grafham Water car park called Mander, at West Perry (GR.144662). This car park is recommended as it has security cameras. A small charge is made for parking.

NB: It is not advisable to use this trail on Bank Holidays as the traffic and bicycle routes will be very busy.

Of Interest:

This ride encompasses the Grafham water Reservoir, which was opened in 1966. One of the woodlands on the northern shore is a SSSI, (Site of Special Scientific Interest), because of its flora and fauna which is typical of ancient woodland. Then, in 1986, the whole reservoir was designated an SSSI because of its wetland birds. Management of the area has attracted dragonflies, butterflies and wild flowers.

Route Description:

Leave the car park and take the metalled road from West Perry heading towards the village of Dillington. *This is a fairly quiet road with private woods on either side.*

After about one mile you will come to a crossroads. Turn left. Keep following the metalled road which narrows into a single track road through the village of Dillington and out the other side. You leave the road at a bend (GR.140651) by going straight on which takes you onto a grass track that forms part of the Three Shires Way. *Make a mental note of the symbol as you will be seeing it again.*

The grass track widens out (GR.144648) and you can enjoy a canter if you wish for 1.25 miles to Midloe Grange. Keeping the Grange on your left (GR.165646) take the track that leads to Highfield Farm Cottages. Do not turn left down the side of the farm. Keep going straight. When the track divides (GR.168661) carry straight on as before. The grass track follows the outside of Diddington Woods where you keep bearing left (GR.173663) to ride down a wide avenue between the woods. *This is a delightful part of the ride in the spring. You are surrounded by Christmas Trees which have a carpet of bluebells. The avenue stretches in front of you, rabbits running away into the woods.*

Towards the end of the woods look carefully for the waymarks (GR.175666); these will point you first right then immediately left to take you over a wooden bridge and out of the wood. Still follow the

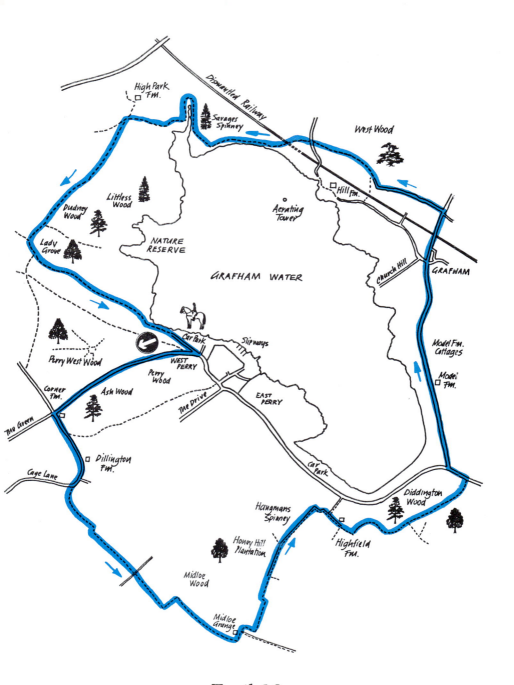

Trail 10

63

sign of the Three Shires Way that takes you to Shooters Hollow Farm Caravan Site (GR.177671). Ride through the caravan site into the farm area itself, and follow the short metalled road out of the farm onto a 'B' road. *Take care here as the road can be very busy.* Turn left onto this road and ride for about 300 yards to the T-junction where you turn right. You now have just over one mile of road work to take you into the village of Grafham. Stay on this road, passing the public house on the right, until you reach the bridleway sign on your left (GR.161697). Follow this bridleway which runs at the back of another caravan site and takes you into West Wood. *Ride carefully in the spring as you have to pick your way through a matting of primula. This wood gets little sunshine so even after a dry spell the bridleway can become boggy in places.*

Turn left (GR.152697) and, as there are no waymarks look for a crossroads of tracks. *If you come to the end of the wood with a wire fence you have gone too far! Turn around and ride back the way you came looking for the first track you see on the right hand side.* When you come out of the wood, turn right and once again you will find the sign of the Three Shires Way.

Turn right (GR.144696) and keep following the track that takes you toward the reservoir. Go through the gate and turn right on to a wide grass verge alongside the cycle route. A short ride on this verge brings you to another gate on your right. Go through this onto a forestry road which takes you through the wood. Just before you come out, follow the bridleway sign to your left down a track that runs down the side of the wood. At the bottom turn right onto another wide grass verge that edges the water. Keep the water on your left as you skirt around it and turn right (GR.132693). In a short distance you rejoin the cycle route. Follow this passing a nature reserve on your left. A grass track takes you to a crossroads of tracks (GR.126690).

Take the left hand track down the side of Littless Wood followed by Dudney Wood and then Lady Grove. At the end of Lady Grove the tracks once more divide (GR.124692). Take the left track which leads back to the car park. The grass track changes (GR.138671) and the last section is ridden on the cycle route. *Please ride with due care and attention for other users.* Go through the gate at the end and you will see your starting place on the left.

Services on this trail include: *Public telephones and public houses at West Perry and Grafham.*

A 13.5 MILE TRAIL (ANTI-CLOCKWISE)

Ordnance Survey Maps:

Pathfinder: 959
Landranger: 141,142 & 153

NB: The A14 Trunk road may not be shown on your map.

Parking & Starting Point:

Parking is available in the village of Keyston at 'The Loop' (GR.044752). Leave the A14 at the junction signposted 'B663 Keyston' and travel southwards along Toll Bar Lane taking first a sharp right hand bend followed by a sharp left hand bend. 'The Loop' is on the right at the southern edge of the village and the area for parking is near the large tree.

Of Interest:

The ride explores, mainly on bridleways, the surprisingly hilly countryside along the Cambridgeshire /Northamptonshire border and follows a ridge route from the Bedfordshire border, which gives extensive northerly views over old Huntingdonshire. It also uses a specially built bridleway bridge over the A14 Trunk Road to explore the area to the north.

Away from the three villages there are few facilities, so it is advisable to take some refreshments with you. The horse-welcoming 'Nags Head' public house at Hargrave provides a convenient half-way stop on the route - note that it does not serve food on Mondays! At Keyston, just after the start, 'The Pheasant' also serves food and there is also a public house/restaurant at Bythorn.

Route Description:

Leave your parking place by riding west up the lane between the bungalow and the chestnut trees. At 'The Pheasant' (GR.043753) go in front of the public house and follow the signposted, public bridleway straight ahead. This becomes a concrete road and goes between buildings which house a turkey farm. At a left turn (GR.037754) the route becomes a rough track beside a private grass landing strip. Just after a small copse, by the waymarker (GR. 036752), turn right on to a grass section keeping the hedge to your right. After reaching a young plantation with an oak tree on your right (GR.033753) turn left and continue to the next junction near some tall coniferous trees (GR.032750). Turn right here and follow the track uphill.

The water from the small brook you have just crossed makes its way along tributary streams into the River Great Ouse 13 miles away at Huntingdon. Yet at this point you are only 3 miles from the River Nene at Denford. The hill that you are about to climb is the watershed or divide between the two river systems that both flow into the North Sea via the Wash.

At the junction (GR.023754) turn left and ride between the high hedges. *You will follow this bridleway for over a mile and it marks the boundary between Cambridgeshire on the left and Northamptonshire to the right. The vegetation each side of the boundary provides a habitat for many forms of wildlife, in contrast to the rather sterile arable fields on each side. The bird song is noticeable in spring and summer. The bridleway, as well as providing a route for humans, also provides a corridor for the movement of wildlife across the countryside. To the left you will notice the spire of Keyston Church and to the right, through a gap, you will see the spire of Raunds Church on the edge of the Nene Valley.*

At the junction with the B663 (GR.026744) continue straight over signposted 'Bridleway to Hargrave'. Notice the Cambridgeshire boundary sign to your left. At the bottom of the valley cross the stream (GR. 034738) and continue round the waymarked barrier and in 60 yards bear to the right following the waymark that is on the Ash tree. *You have now ridden into Northamptonshire.* **Follow the route just inside the wood until you reach the most southerly corner (GR.035727). Turn right still following the waymarker. You are now once again riding along the county boundary with a hedge to your left and an arable field to your right.**

Follow the signposted route 'Bridleway to Covington' (GR 034725). Turn right (GR.038724) back into Northamptonshire following the rough track with the hedge to the right. After 175 yards at a gap in the hedge (GR.038723) turn right and ride for 0.6 miles until you reach the double metal gates (GR.033716) Continue straight on going through the bridlegate to the left.

Here you go over the remains of the dismantled Huntingdon, Thrapston and Kettering railway line whose embankment still dominates the landscape.

On the other side of the 'track immediately turn left, following the waymarker through the gate with old railway 'SHUT AND FASTEN' sign and then go diagonally right towards the double gates at Bottom Farm. Turn left onto the metalled road and follow the appropriately named Brook Street. At the T-junction (GR.033708) turn left and ride into the village of Hargrave.

Take care at the blind corner to the right. There are no verges, but Church Street is a quiet road.

The quiet village of Hargrave, whose name means Hare Grove, is fortunately just off the busy A45. Its church of All Saints has an attractive 13th century porch and an unusual coffin on the north side. During an excavation in 1893 into an Iron Age and Roman Settlement to the north of the village (GR.035722), a coffin was found with 'a man's bones'. After the excavation the bones were replaced in the coffin and placed in the churchyard.

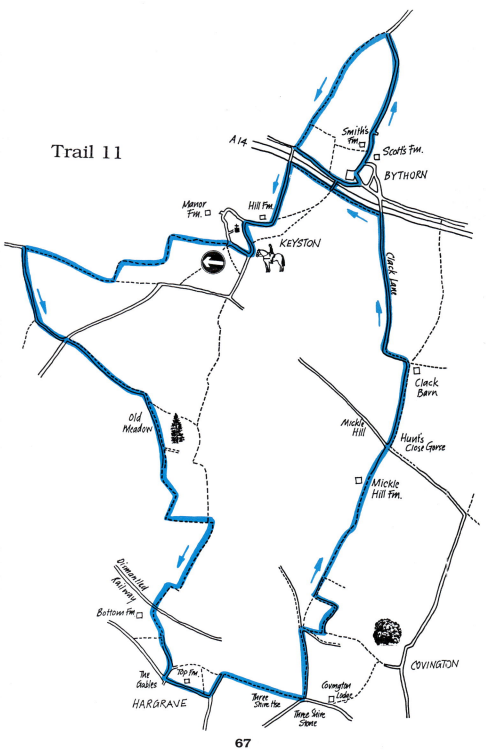

Trail 11

A 14

Smith's Fm.

Scott's Fm.

BYTHORN

Manor Fm.

Hill Fm.

KEYSTON

Clack Lane

Clack Barn

Mickle Hill

Hunt's Close Gorse

Mickle Hill Fm.

Old Meadow

Dismantled Railway

Bottom Fm.

The Gables

Top Fm.

HARGRAVE

Three Shire Hse

Three Shire Stone

Covington Lodge

COVINGTON

At the 'Nag's Head' Public House (GR.036707), opposite the church, turn left signposted 'No through road'. Turn right (GR.038708) onto a public bridleway and ride towards the water tower, going through an area of overgrown hedge before you reach the A45 (GR.046705) and a bridleway signpost.

On the other side of the road is the 'Three Counties Stone' marking the meeting point of Bedfordshire, Northamptonshire and Cambridge shire (Huntingdonshire is written on the stone).

Turn left following the bridleway sign 'Bridleway to Keyston', keeping to the grass verge. Turn left through the house yard and ride to the right of the garage following the waymark. After the waymarker (GR.047713), turn right following further waymarkers and cross the field towards the signpost (GR.048713). Turn left signposted 'Public Bridleway' and follow the gravel track through the derelict farm buildings. Continue along the track to meet the hedge (GR.051714) where you bear left, keeping the hedge on your right going downhill. The bridleway turns sharp right (GR.048716) and goes towards Muckle Hill Farm, whose roofs appear above the hill.

From here you ride along the top of a steep sided ridge with distant views. Ahead is the A14 Trunk Road linking the M1 with the A1 and the East Coast Ports. Beyond the A14 is the village of Bythorn its church having a truncated spire. To the left is the larger spire of Keyston Church and further to the left is the fine spire of Raunds Parish Church.

Keep the hedge to the right. Go through the hedge on the right (GR.053723) and continue in the same direction with the hedge to the left. Just before the corner (GR.054724) turn left under an ash tree and then right and follow the hedge boundary to the left with Mickle Hill Farm ahead. From the farm (GR.054727) continue straight onto the metalled surface. At the junction with the highway at Hunt's Close Gorse (GR. 057731), go straight over signposted 'Public Bridleway - Bythorn 2' to Clack Barn (GR.059738). Go in front of the farm buildings and turn left downhill over a stream onto Clack Lane.

Here the scene becomes pastoral with sheep grazing in the valley bottom. This has preserved a vast area of mediaeval cultivation remains on both sides of Clack Lane between here and the A14. You can see the ridge and furrow of part of the old field system of Bythorn and Keyston. Unlike most villages, Keyston was not all enclosed at the same time. To the south of the parish the land was owned by the Duke of Manchester, who was keen to get rid of the old field system, but to the north the land was outside his ownership and the old system of narrow strip fields was not removed until 1850. It is the extensive remains of these fields we see today in this valley.

On reaching the A14 (GR.057755) turn left onto the new concrete bridleway running parallel to the A14 and make for the bridleway bridge (GR.054757).

At this point it is possible to shorten the route by two miles by continuing straight on.

At the bridge turn right and cross the dual carriageway. At the T-junction (GR.054758) turn right into the village of Bythorn. After approximately 250 yards turn into Warren Lane (GR.056758).

On your right you will see St Lawrence's Church described in one book as 'an unhappy sight' with most of its spire removed and an unusual cap in its place.

At Smith's Lane continue straight on and follow the public byway sign. *Along this track on the right is a weed-covered piece of old farm machinery mainly made of wood. Words cast into a metal wheel tell you it is a hay loader. It has obviously been here for many years.*

At the T-junction (GR.059774) turn left onto a grass bridleway.

Once again we reach the border of Cambridgeshire and there are views westwards into Northamptonshire and the Nene Valley. Clopton Hall can be seen among the trees to the north-west. A quiet isolated spot, except for the traffic noise from the A14!

Ahead you will see the spire of Keyston Church, near your finishing point. At the metalled road (GR.049763) turn left. *This used to be the main road between Huntingdon and Thrapston (A604) before being replaced by the A14. The building to the right was a garage and roadside cafe.* **Continue along this road to turn right (GR.054758) and re-cross the bridleway bridge over the A14.**

The shortened route rejoins here.

On reaching the southern side (GR.054757), turn right and follow the concrete bridleway parallel to the A14 in a north westerly direction. At the end of the bridleway go through the metal gates and turn left into Toll Bar Lane (GR.048760). *Take care at this junction and look out for traffic coming from the right.*

Follow the road through Keyston taking a sharp right hand bend and then a sharp left hand bend by a notice board and telephone kiosk.

These bends take the road around the large area of a moated site and other earthworks (GR.046753), which are probably the original defensive site of Keyston, with Toll Bar Lane going straight towards the north east corner of the moat. The modern village has grown-up around the edge of the old site.

Continue down the hill, passing the parish church on the right, until you reach your parking place at 'The Loop'.

ACROSS THE CAUSEWAY FROM WILLINGHAM TO ALDRETH

TRAIL 12

**A 10.5 MILE RIDING & DRIVING TRAIL
(FIGURE OF EIGHT)**

Ordnance Survey Maps:
Pathfinder: 961
Landranger: 154

Parking & Starting Point:
Parking is available in Willingham on the tarmac car park on the green at the junction of Church Road, Rockmill End, Iram Drove and Green Road (GR.408705). You will see the green by the old village pump and the village sign. **Please note that it is important to remove all litter and droppings from the tarmac area and, by order of the Parish Council, it is forbidden to exercise your horse or dog on the green.**

Willingham is best approached by leaving the A14 Trunk road (still the A604 on older maps) at Bar Hill (GR.383640) and taking the B1050 to Willingham via Longstanton. At Willingham Co-operative on the left (GR.404705) turn right into Church Road and, after passing the Parish Church of St Mary and All Saints, the green is a further 400 metres on the right.

Of Interest:
The route follows mainly public byways with a short distance on quiet, minor unclassified roads. There are no gates on the route. The surfaces are good, but in a few places there are passable ruts. The time of year you travel this route should be taken into consideration. There are excellent facilities in Willingham for the purchase of food. Refreshments are available near the end of the route at The Milk Maid public house at Rampton End (GR.408702), which has a narrow entrance, but good horse/carriage parking. 'The Duke of Wellington' in Church Road near the starting point has similar facilities.

Trail 12

Sponge Drove

Meadow Drove

WILLINGHAM

Iram Drove

The Stacks

The Causeway

Tibbits Fm

Hempsal's Road

Belsar's Hill Settlement

70

There are no opportunities on the route for the purchase of food or drink once you leave Willingham. There is a public telephone at Aldreth.

This trail explores the old route across

Willingham's key position on this route led to the parish church being, from 1340, a place where large ordination services were held admitting sometimes over 200 candidates to Holy Orders. The

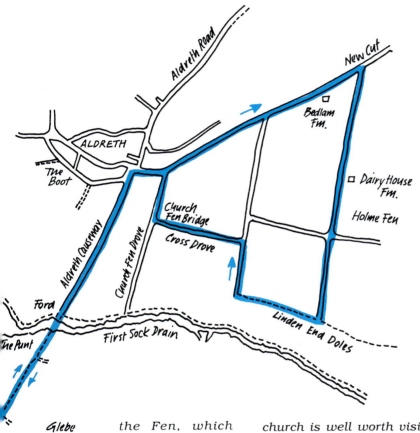

the Fen, which was in medieval times the only carriage route from the fen-edge at Willingham across to the fen isle at Haddenham and thence to the Isle of Ely. Those riding and driving this trail will be following in the footsteps of kings and bishops, who undertook this dangerous journey.

church is well worth visiting for its medieval wall paintings, which date from the mid-thirteenth century and show a 300 year sequence from that date.

Willingham is a large village with a population of over 3000 people and has shopping facilities matching a village of that size. It grew rapidly in the 19th century when the demand for agricultural produce meant that hard and soft fruit, asparagus and flowers were sent to Covent Garden from Longstanton Station. Although the area now grows root and grain crops on its farms, the market garden/smallholding tradition still survives and many bargains can be had from the produce stalls along the Longstanton Road.

Route Description:

Leave your parking place by the entrance and turn left into Green Street. At the junction continue straight over into Rockmill End, keeping the Public Library on your left. At the junction with Sponge Drove (GR.409707) turn right, signposted 'Meadow Road (but Drove on the map) leading to Tibbit's, Glebe, Hempsal and Norris's Farms', and ride for approximately 1 mile to The Stacks (GR.426707). Bear left here following the metalled road for 120 yards and then, as the metalled road bears right, continue straight on to 'The Causeway (Track)' (GR.427708).

This causeway leads across the fen to a crossing point of the River Great Ouse and then follows the 'Aldreth Causeway' to the village of Aldreth. The word 'causeway' on a map often indicates an ancient route and there is evidence, that beneath this route across the fen there lies a Late Bronze Age timber track linking Willingham and Aldreth.

In medieval times the Aldreth Causeway, built in the early 12th century to reach the Abbey at Ely, was part of the only carriage route from Cambridge across the undrained fen to Ely and remained so until 1754. As you make your way along

the Causeway you will see straight ahead the sails of the Great Mill - a brick tower mill built in 1803, which lies on the ridge between Haddenham and Aldreth. The water tower and communications mast are situated in the centre of Haddenham.

Bear right (GR.435718) and continue on the causeway until you reach the bridge (GR.437722). At this point 'The Causeway' crosses the River Great Ouse which makes its roundabout way across the Fens from Earith to Ely. This sluggish course caused the badly drained Fens to exist and in the 17th century two straight cuts were made from Earith to near Kings Lynn to improve the drainage of this area enabling the great reclamation schemes to take place. To cross the bridge the road diverts slightly to the right and a more direct route would take you to the ford, which was the first method of crossing the river. To the right, high banks called 'levees' can be seen each side of the river.

Continue along the track parallel to the Catchwater Drain to the entrance to Aldreth (GR.444733). Turn right onto the metalled road - signposted Public Byway. After 250 yards bear left onto the public byway - signposted at the last turn. This is a fen edge route around the fen island of Haddenham following the New Cut (Drain). Many of the farms in this area are deserted; their owners having moved into the villages years ago. **After riding for about one mile to a point just after Bedlam Farm (GR.462737), turn right onto Dairy House Drove and ride into Holme Fen.**

Ahead you can see the tower of Cottenham Church and the arable *landscape around you grows wheat, sugar beet, barley and potatoes. In the summer you will sometimes see a field of bright blue linseed. The blue flowers close and disappear when the light fades leaving you wondering where you have previously seen it!*

At the metalled road (GR.456726) continue straight across to the T-junction (GR.456719) where you turn right onto the grassy Linden End Doles (Track).

Agriculturally, doles indicate an area of land shared out yearly among the parishioners. The land was doled out each year and the word 'dole' has subsequently changed its meaning and become, in modern times, money given to the unemployed. Across to the left are the old buildings of the Smithy Fen Engine Pumping Station and the bank of the drainage channel. This shows how the land, at about one metre about sea level, is much lower than the main water course and pumps are needed to raise the water into them.

At the old willow tree and waymarker (GR.451723) turn right into Lakes Drove (Track). On meeting the metalled road (GR.452726), turn left into Cross Drove and continue until you reach the T-junction at Church Fen Bridge (GR.444728). Turn right, crossing the Haddenham Fen Drain and ride towards Aldreth. Bear left (GR.446732) into Aldreth. *The village is built at the end of a long tongue of land*

where the Causeway reaches the higher land.

Turn left (GR.444733) and return back along the Causeway to the bridge across the river (GR.437722). *To the left of the bridge on the northern bank is a triangular pillar, or trig point. These were used by Ordnance Survey as fixed points with known heights to map the countryside in large triangles. Even at this low-lying spot this pillar could be seen from quite a distance. The grooves on the top used to hold a theodolite. The pillars have been made obsolete with the coming of satellite mapping. Note the name of the iron foundry - Nickerson, Eagle Works, Ely on the bridge posts.*

Continue along the Causeway to Tibbit's Farm (GR.427708) where you bear right along the metalled road for 120 metres and then continue onto the public byway between the hedges. *The byway starts to cross Belsar's Hill (GR.424704) which is a nearly circular prehistoric earthwork/settlement 400 yards long and 325 yards wide with a bank and ditch. The Causeway leads directly to the earthwork and seems to have a connection with it. Views of the earthwork can be seen on both sides of the hedge.*

At the metalled Iram Drove (GR.422701) turn right and ride the mile to your parking place at Willingham.

A 13.5 MILE CIRCULAR RIDING & DRIVING TRAIL

Ordnance Survey Maps:
Pathfinder: 878, 879, 898 & 899
Landranger: 131 & 143

Parking & Starting Point:
Parking is available by kind permission of the Playing Field Committee, at the Gorefield Playing Field Car Park in Wolf Lane (GR.422117). Please turn left on entering the car park and park on the gravel away from the Bowls Club building. ***It is important to remove all litter and droppings from the area before leaving.***

Gorefield Playing Field Car Park is best approached by leaving the B1169 at Leverington Common, Wolf Lane (GR.423098) and travelling northwards, signposted 'Gorefield'. In approximately one mile you will see the car park on your right.

Of Interest:
The route follows mainly grass and metalled byways and minor unclassified roads and there are no gates. At Leverington Common it is necessary to go along the B1169 for 200 yards. The surfaces are generally good and in many places excellent, but one should always take into account the time of the year and the weather conditions.

There are no facilities available along the route and you should take your own food and drink. In Gorefield there is a general stores/post office/petrol station and a public house serving food. There are public telephones at Gorefield and Harold's Bridge.

This area is just to the west of the medieval sea bank which protected the area from flooding and allowed the marsh to be drained in the 14th and 15th centuries. Sometimes the sea bank, which can be seen near Leverington (GR.447108), is called the Roman Bank, but although scholars have argued over the dating of these first efforts to protect this area, it is generally accepted that it was built in the Middle Ages. On this trail you will see examples of the latest engineering technology that ensures the fens are kept from flooding.

Route Description:

Leave the car park and turn right onto the metalled Wolf Lane. At the T-junction turn right and travel eastwards out of Gorefield. At Cherrytree Farm, (GR.426117), turn left on to the public byway between the farm and a house where the surface becomes a grassy track.

On meeting the metalled road near Fitton Hall (GR.430126), turn left and after 50 yards turn left onto an unsigned public byway opposite the entrance to Fitton Hall.

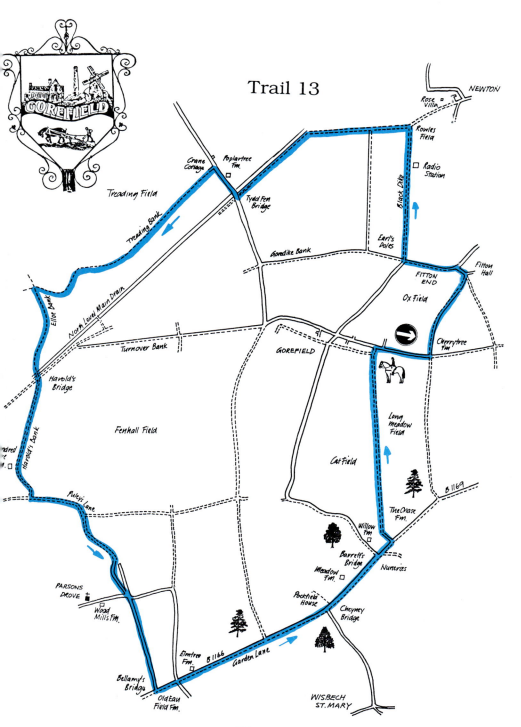

Trail 13

NEWTON

Rose Villa

Radio Station

Rowles Field

GOREFIELD

Crane Cottage

Poplartree Fm.

Treading Field

Tydd Fen Bridge

Treading Bank

Goredike Bank

Black Dike

Earl's Poles

FITTON END

Fitton Hall

Elliot Bank

North Level Main Drain

Ox Field

Turnover Bank

GOREFIELD

Cherrytree Fm.

Harold's Bridge

Long meadow Field

Fenhall Field

Cat Field

B 1169

Harold's Bank

The Chase Fm.

Puleys Lane

Willow Fm.

Barrett's Bridge

Nurseries

Meadow Fm.

PARSONS DROVE

Pocktield House

Cheyney Bridge

Wood Mills Fm.

Elmtree Fm.

B 1166

Garden Lane

Bellamy's Bridge

Old Eau Field Fm.

WISBECH ST. MARY

Around Wisbech roses are grown in the silty soils and you will see large fields of them and rose rootstock. **Continue straight on at Oxfield House until you reach the metalled road (GR.423127). Turn right and go straight across the road that runs parallel to the previous byway into the sign posted public byway called Black Dyke. Continue on towards the British Telecom communications mast.**

At this point, the fields on either side of the trail were drained in the 14th and 15th centuries and are now about 6 feet above sea level. They were drained in large areas of between 50 and 200 acres and you will notice the names of these fields on the 1:25000 maps. In fact, the fields on the right were drained in 1395 and the fields on the left a little later in 1438. This area is not a major bulb-growing area like Spalding to the north-east, but sometimes you will see a field of daffodils and tulips in flower in the spring. Bulbs grow well in the silty soils. Peas are another crop grown in this area and these are for canning and freezing.

At the mast (GR.424138) the surface becomes metalled until the T-junction at Rowles Field (GR.424143). At the T-junction, turn left past the 'Bungalow' and where the metalled road turns sharp left (GR.420142), continue straight onto the signposted public byway and go under the electricity transmission lines. Do not turn left at the next junction (GR.413142), but continue straight making towards the cog-wheeled sluice gate. Turn left here

onto the byway by the North Level Main Drain, which should now be on your right.

The eight mile long North Level Main Drain, built between 1831 and 1834 to go straight between Clough's Cross and Tydd, replaced the Shire Drain which took a tortuous route of 10 miles between the same places. Today the Cambridgeshire /Lincolnshire border still follows the route of the old Shire Drain. The Shire Drain was part of Vermuyden's 1630 scheme to drain the North Level. Examples of modern automatic electric pumps can be seen both sides of Tydd Fen Bridge.

On reaching the metalled road by the bridge (GR.406134), turn right over the bridge and follow the metalled road past Poplar Tree Farm on your right   Turn left at Crane Cottage (GR.404137) onto a narrow metalled road. At the end of the metalled section (GR. 396129) continue on to the signposted public byway called Treading Bank. The byway takes a winding course towards and away from the electricity transmission lines on your right. When you come close to the lines for the second time (GR.386124), turn left on to Elloe Bank. This eventually becomes a metalled road. You will pass some cottages on your right (GR.387117).

Behind these cottages is a small waterway called Lady Nunn's Old Eau, which is the southern part of the old Shire Drain. The cottages are in Cambridgeshire, but the fields and farm beyond are in Lincolnshire. A little to the north of here on the Shire Drain near Sutton St Edmund

(GR.384132), where the first steam engine for drainage purposes was built and put into operation in about 1817. This had a short life because it no longer served a useful purpose after the North Level Main Drain by-passed it in 1834.

Cross Harold's Bridge (GR.387114) and turn right. *Over to the left you can see the Harold's Bridge Primitive Methodist Chapel built in 1908 and now closed. Primitive Methodism had a strong following in agricultural communities and their chapels were built in many small settlements in the Fens. The foundation stones of this chapel are a testimony to the enthusiasm of this community just after the turn of the century. The chapel is used now as a 'chitting' shed. In the early part of the year seed potatoes are kept in warm, frost-free conditions to encourage the shoots to grow or 'chit' from the eyes so that they can 'get-away' quickly after planting around Eastertime. Potatoes are an important crop in this area.*

Follow the metalled unclassified road past Hundred Acre Farm on your right. As the road bends to the right (GR.387103), take the grass-surfaced signposted public byway to the left called 'Pulley's Lane'. Where Pulley's Lane goes left (GR.393100), you go straight on, keeping the ditch to your right. The track enters a small settlement at the back of the houses and reaches the metalled road at Glebe Lodge (GR.397093). **Turn right into Elbow Lane and within a few yards you reach the B1166. Bear to the left of the island and go straight across to the signposted public byway opposite.**

Take care here as there is a blind bend to the left.

Drive to the T-junction at the metalled road near Old Eau Field Farm and turn left towards Bellamy's Bridge (GR.402084). Turn right here, signposted 'Guyhirn 4' and then immediately go left along the road in front of the row of semi-detached houses. *If you wait for the right moment at this crossing it is possible to do the turn without going on to the B1169.*

Follow this quiet, unclassified road called Garden Lane, which runs parallel to the B1169, until you reach a road crossing at Cheyney Bridge (GR.417092). *On each side you see orchards. The Wisbech area has always specialised in the growing of hard and soft fruit and the area is especially attractive in blossom time. Do not be tempted to turn right to the 'Railway Bell', as it is much further than indicated on the sign and is not open at lunch time on weekdays!*

Continue straight over the road and drive on to Panswell Lane/Barrett's Bridge (GR. 423097). Turn left and then right - signposted 'Wisbech 2 B1169, Leverington 1' to travel along the B1169 for 200 yards. At Wolf Lane (GR.423098), turn left - signposted 'Gorefield'. After passing through orchards for about one mile, you will see your parking place on the right.

A 5 MILE CIRCULAR TRAIL (ANTI-CLOCKWISE)

Ordnance Survey Maps:
Landranger: 142
Pathfinder: 897

NB: Due to diversions, parts of this route may not be as shown on your Ordnance Survey maps.

Parking & Starting Point:
Parking is available on the grass verge just after the track to Woodcroft Lodge and Pellett Hall (GR.139035). From the A47 west of Peterborough, take the road signposted 'Castor' and from there the road signposted 'Marholm'. When you reach Marholm go straight over the crossroads into Woodcroft Road. Take the next turn left signposted 'Etton; and continue straight along the road until it bears sharp right. You will find a suitable parking place here.

Route Description:

From your parking place continue along the grass verges of this narrow country road for approximately one mile. *You will pass Woodcroft Castle on your right. This is late 13th century with later alterations and additions. It has a stout circular tower either side of the front and a gateway in the middle. It would probably have had a courtyard and two more towers similar to Barnwell and Harlech Castles when it was built.*

When you reach Spring Cottages, bear left and continue on the track.

From Maxhams Cottage (GR. 135045) follow the bridleway sign along the wide hard track. *There is a good view to the right across acres of farm land. Ahead and to the left you can see the village of Helpston. Here the poet John Clare was born on 13th July 1793 to extremely poor parents. Their cottage was one of the narrowest and wretched of the hundred or so mud cottages which made up Helpston at that time. Helpston got its name from a Helpo, or stipendiary knight, who practised his craft here in Norman times. The name remained long after he had gone. Before the Normans, however, there had been a large and important Roman settlement, a Durobrivae. Their roads are still used today to get from one village to another in this region on the edge of the Fens.*

Continue straight along this track for approximately 0.6 miles, until you get to a Torpel Way sign where you turn left (GR.125044). This is a wide grassy track which runs for the length of Oxey Wood and you continue riding along it for about 0.8 miles, keeping the edge of the wood on your right. *There is a deep ditch between the track and the wood which is overgrown in places and difficult to see.*

Where Oxey Wood meets Simons Wood (GR.125034) the track bears left and then right around the end of the wood, it then carries straight on again. Bear right (GR.128033) going around the corner of the wood and then continue up the side of the wood. After about 180 yards

At the end of the wood the track goes through a hedge and over a small bridge, it then turns left up the side of the hedge. Follow this until you come to a hard track and turn right here. *There may be bee-hives along this route in the spring and summer.* At the end of the track, near the farm buildings, you meet the road. Turn left to come back to your parking place.

It is sometimes possible to park in Marholm, just inside Woodcroft Road on a wide part of the verge. This is just round the corner from the Fitzwilliam Arms public house where you can obtain a very nice meal. Its name comes from the Fitzwilliam family who own Milton Estate and a lot of land in this area.

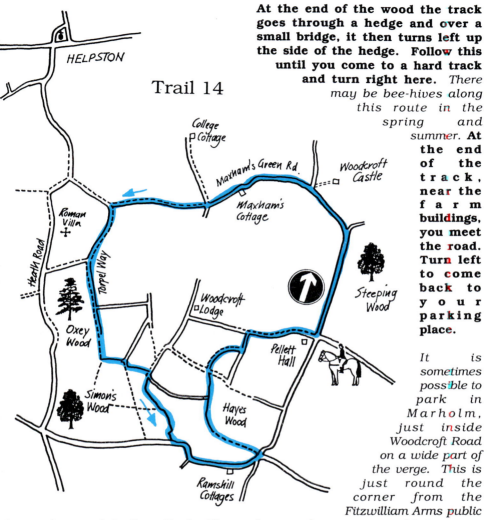

HELPSTON

Trail 14

College Cottage

Maxham's Green Rd.

Woodcroft Castle

Maxham's Cottage

Roman Villa

Heath Road

Torpel Way

Woodcroft Lodge

Steeping Wood

Oxey Wood

Pellett Hall

Simon's Wood

Hayes Wood

Ramshill Cottages

the track turns left along the inside of the road hedge (GR.130028). Follow this track until it reaches Hayes Wood where it turns left. Ride along this keeping the wood on your right.

If you look carefully you can see deer tracks going through the woods and some of the trees in the middle of the fields have rubbing marks on the trunks where the stags have rubbed their antlers.

79

THE BREWERS LOOP

A 10 MILE CIRCULAR TRAIL (ANTI-CLOCKWISE)

Ordnance Survey Maps:
Landranger: 153
Pathfinder: 1026

Parking & Starting Points:
Parking is available in the wide entrance to the byway (GR.276411) which is half way along the road from Ashwell to Steeple Morden. This is also your starting point.

Route Description:

From your parking place head southwards down the unmarked byway for about 0.75 miles to Ashwell Street which is an old Roman road. At the Crossways (GR.282402), turn left and ride for about 3 miles along the track known as Ashwell Street, crossing Station Road (GR.289407). You will pass High Farm on the left and the Hill Plantation on the right before coming to Upper Gatley End and then on to ride through very open countryside which surrounds the old wartime airfield at Steeple Morden to the north.

Turn left onto the road (GR.317421), and ride into Litlington village. Follow the village street passing the Crown Public House and head towards the church. Turn right (GR.309427) to Abington Piggotts. Follow this lane using the wide grass verges and ride down into the valley.

After crossing the stream and leaving the woodland, turn left (GR.308440) on the farm road to Down Hall Farm. After 0.25 miles, turn right on to the bridleway, on a stone track. Follow this as it bears left, and, where the track splits (GR.301440), ride straight ahead following the blue waymarker. You will see some buildings straight ahead in the distance. The track eventually becomes grassy and joins a tarmac road (GR.292434). Follow this road and turn right to ride past the houses on your left, heading for the crossroads at the end of Bogs Gap Lane.

Go straight across into Trap Road (GR.287433), towards Guilden Morden. After 0.25 miles, the road bends right, and the byway leads off to the left, by a large metal gate. Follow the byway uphill towards Guilden Morden, and at the end of Buxtons Lane (GR.278435) turn right along the peaceful High Street.

Immediately before the Three Tuns public house, turn left into Silver Street (GR.278437) and follow the bridleway into open country and downhill across the Hertfordshire County border. Rejoin the small farm track by a ditch (GR.271428) and follow it to Northfield Road (GR.264430) and turn left.

Follow this lane for about 1.75 miles. **DO NOT USE THE CROSS COUNTRY JUMPS IN THE FIELD ON THE RIGHT.**

At the junction on the outskirts of Ashwell (GR.270401), turn left and ride uphill for 0.75 miles back to your starting point.

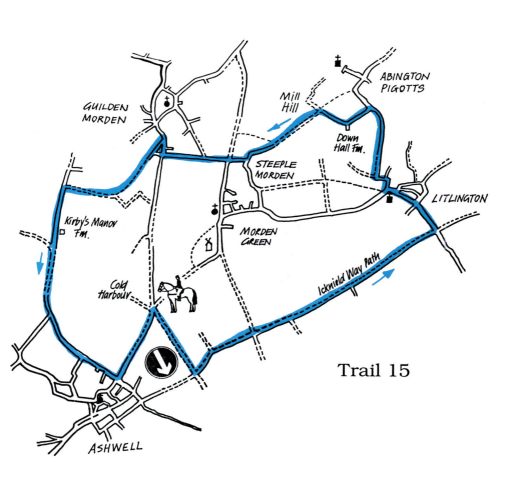

Trail 15

BED & BREAKFAST FOR HORSES

*AN ESSENTIAL DIRECTORY WHEN PLANNING
A RIDING HOLIDAY*

£4.95 (inc. p&p)

from:

BHS Book and Gift Shop
Stoneleigh Park, Kenilworth, Warwickshire CV8 2LR

Registered Charity No 210504

A 13 MILE CIRCULAR TRAIL (CLOCKWISE)

Ordnance Survey Maps:
Pathfinder: 1003
Landranger: 154

Parking & Starting Point:
Parking is available on the wide grass verge, just past the disused railway bridge (GR.300537). Your route is described from this point. Additional parking is available on the road side on the outskirts of Longstowe (GR.305541).

Of Interest:
This ride goes through Hayley Wood which is a Site of Special Scientific Interest (SSSI). This is a wet wood and has been a nature reserve since 1962. Please do not pick or collect any flowers, even common ones.

The wood dates back 800 years and is first mentioned by name in the Ely Coucher Book, a record of the possessions of the Bishop of Ely in 1251, and from this time its history is well documented. In 1356 the Bishop of Ely was on the run for murder, and the king seized his estates. They were handed on to others until Queen Elizabeth confiscated and sold the wood in 1602. It then passed through a long succession of owners before the Wildlife Trust purchased it.

You will find lots of butterflies and other insects which feed on valerian, clustered bell-flower and greater burnet-saxifrage and the rare oxlip growing in the wood alongside bluebells, wood anemones and dog's mercury.

Longstowe village has one public house, named after The Golden Miller. Various memorabilia is on display as this local horse won the 1934 Grand National. It also won the Gold Cup in 1932, 1933, 1934, 1935 and 1936. To date he is the only horse to have won both races in the same year. Coming from Ireland in 1930, he was trained by a local man, Basil Briscoe, in the meadow opposite the pub. The stable block he was housed in still exists, a few yards away. There is a small car park at the rear of the pub - check for spaces before driving in.

Route Description:

From your parking place ride down the road away from Longstowe. You will see a water tower ahead on the right hand side of the road. Just past here (GR.294537) turn left onto the bridleway going into Hayley Wood.

When the track leaves the wood (GR.296527) turn right and ride along the outskirts of the wood, crossing a wooden bridge (GR. 293527). Follow this track along the edge of the wood keeping the ditch to your right until the track divides (GR.289525). Take the track straight ahead towards the barn leaving the wood behind. Follow the bridleway to the left of the barn and turn left (GR.287525)

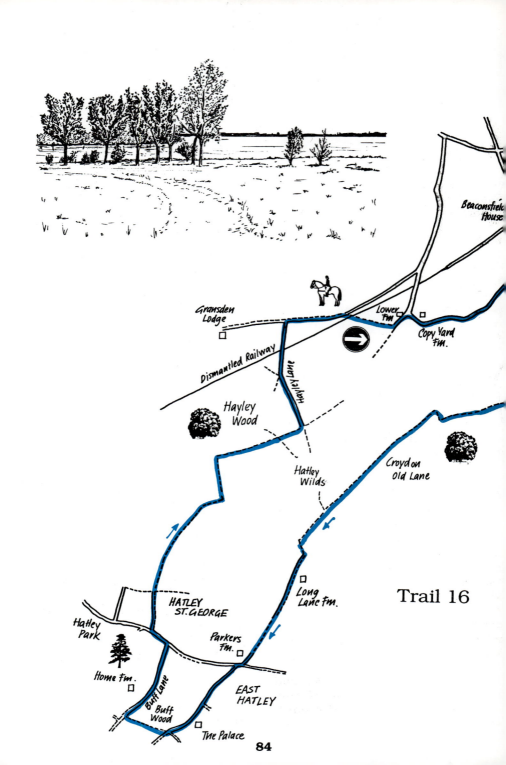

Beaconsfield House

Gransden Lodge

Lower Fm.

Copy Yard Fm.

Dismantled Railway

Hayley Lane

Hayley Wood

Hatley Wilds

Croydon Old Lane

Long Lane Fm.

Trail 16

HATLEY ST. GEORGE

Hatley Park

Parkers Fm.

Home Fm.

Buff Lane

Buff Wood

EAST HATLEY

The Palace

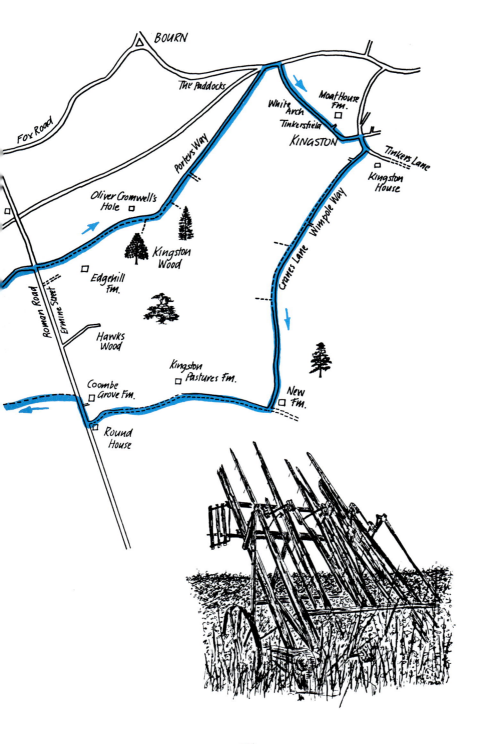

BOURN

The Paddocks

Fox Road

White Arch

Moat House Fm.

Tinkersfield

KINGSTON

Tinkers Lane

Porters Way

Kingston House

Oliver Cromwell's Hole

Kingston Wood

Cranes Lane

Wimpole Way

Edgehill Fm.

Roman Road

Ermine Street

Hawks Wood

Kingston Pastures Fm.

Coombe Grove Fm.

New Fm.

Round House

85

taking the grass tack at the left side of the concrete farm road which goes slightly uphill.

At the point where the concrete road ends, the track splits into two (GR.288522). Turn right here heading towards Hatley village. Ride with the ditch to your left and after 200 yards cross the track so that the ditch is on your right hand side. Follow this track until it gradually becomes a gravel farm track and joins the road in Hatley village (GR.282510). Turn left. Pass the village green on your right and join the Buff Lane bridleway on your right (GR.282509).

Follow this surfaced road and turn left (GR.279503) to follow the edge of Buff Wood. At the top of the short slope, go through the small wooden fence between the Wood and The Barn, and turn left (GR.283501) and follow the track which eventually becomes a road. Rejoin the road in Hatley (GR. 288507), turning right, and join the bridleway on the left at Parkers Farm (GR.289507). Follow this farm track for about 0.75 miles going through the small gate (GR.295517) and continuing straight ahead.

On reaching the stony track (GR.297520) turn right and follow this track until it turns right (GR.299522). At this point take the narrow bridleway into the wood. Follow this bridleway through the wood (GR.307528) to leave and cross a small wooden bridge, turning immediately right. Follow this track around the edge of the field and head towards the A1198 road (GR.320529)(formerly the A14) APPROACH WITH CARE; FAST TRAFFIC USES THIS ROAD.

Leave the field by the wooden bridge and turn right. Ridge along the good wide grass verge for 50 yards to turn left along the road by the dog kennels (GR.321527). This is signposted to Old Wimpole.

Follow this road to turn left on to the narrow bridleway (GR.337527), part of the Wimpole Way, immediately before the farm. Follow Cranes Lane, part of the Wimpole Way, into Kingston and at the T-junction (GR.346550) turn left towards the crossroads.

At the crossroads turn left and follow this road to a T-junction (GR.339558) and turn left again. In 100 yards ahead on the left hand side is Porters Way. Join this well used track (GR.338558) and follow it until it meets the A1198 (GR.338541). *Approach this point with care, this road carries fast moving traffic.* Cross straight over and continue along the wide grass track, past the Red House public house on your left and where the track narrows into a stony lane (GR.306536) turn right passing Copy Yard Farm on the right. At the end of the narrow section* turn left and after 100 yards (GR. 304536) turn right and follow the wide grass track back over the disused railway bridge to your parking place.

If you wish to visit the Golden Miller, turn right here onto the concrete track. Ride on passing Bellams Farm on the right, until you meet the B1046 and turn right. You are now about one mile from the Golden Miller.

SAFETY

Know your Highway Code (1994 Edition)

In Particular Paragraphs 216/224

RIDE WITH:

CARE

- *For the Land*

COURTESY

- *To other users*

CONSIDERATION

- *For the Farmer*

DISCLAIMER

Whilst all due care was taken in the preparation of these maps neither the British Horse Society nor their agents or servants accept any responsibility for any inaccuracies which may occur. It should be borne in mind that landmarks and conditions change and it is assumed that the user has a Pathfinder or Landranger Ordnance Survey map and a compass.

The Country Code should be observed by every rider, with great care being taken to keep to the line of the Public Rights of Way Particularly when crossing farmland

KINGSTON

**TRAIL
17**

A 12 MILE CIRCULAR TRAIL (ANTI-CLOCKWISE)

Ordnance Survey Maps:
Pathfinder: 1003
Landranger: 154

Parking & Starting Point:
From the A603, follow the signs for Wimpole Hall. Park on the wide verge opposite the entrance. Please take care not to obstruct the route across the verge indicated by the tracks, this is used by the heavy horses from Wimpole Farm.

Of Interest:
Wimpole Hall is owned by the National Trust who have generously provided additional permissive riding tracks around their grounds which are open between April and October.

Riders wishing to use these tracks should apply for permission, in advance, to the Property Manager at Wimpole Hall; you will also be given details of additional parking available to those using the permissive tracks. A leaflet giving full details is available from the Ticket Office.

Please note that these tracks are in constant use by visitors to Wimpole Hall, many of whom will not be used to horses. You are urgently requested to respect this fact when using them and to please walk when near to other users. You should also note that you may be held responsible for any damage you make and that if you do NOT have a permit then you may be asked to leave the grounds.

Trail 17

Route Description:

From your starting place on the grass verge ride north along the road passing Wimpole Hall Farm on your left. The route takes you slightly uphill where you turn right (GR.339526) onto the bridleway to ride through trees.

Follow the Mare Way bridleway, passing the reservoir (GR.353525) and continue riding straight ahead until you come to a grass track on your left (GR.364517). Turn left here.

88

Continue along the grass track which eventually becomes gravel and ride on down hill, passing the disused quarry on the left (GR.367520). Continue on to turn left (GR.369523), over the brow of the hill to rejoin the road (GR. 372528). Turn left, onto the road.

Ride for a short distance and turn left (GR.369531) onto the Mare Way bridleway, and follow this track uphill and bear left, then right as the track follows the line of trees. Ride straight ahead uphill to turn right on the bridleway (GR. 363520). *This is a high point along the route and there are good views of the countryside from here.*

Follow the bridleway and turn right immediately before the reservoir onto a gravel farm track (GR.353525). Ride downhill.

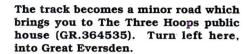

The track becomes a minor road which brings you to The Three Hoops public house (GR.364535). Turn left here, into Great Eversden.

Continue your ride going through the village, following the road as it bends right and then left, past a pig farm to your left (GR.363541) and continue along the road, Tinkers Lane, uphill into Kingston.

Turn left into Cranes Lane (GR. 346550). This surfaced road leads onto a wide byway. Continue riding straight ahead. *Please do not be tempted to use the tracks on either side, these are available to licensed riders only who have bought a permit from South Sea Farms, Kingston.* Follow this track until you rejoin the road next to New Farm (GR.337527) and turn left.

After 500 yards the road bends right and you continue to follow it back to your parking place.

There is an alternative ride for those who have arranged to use the permissive tracks in Wimpole Hall. The route is shown on the leaflet which can be purchased from the Ticket Office at Wimpole Hall. If you do not have a permit then you may be asked to leave the grounds. Please also note that you could be held responsible for any damage you commit.

NOTE: AS THESE TRACKS ARE IN CONSTANT USE BY VISITORS TO WIMPOLE HALL, MANY OF WHOM WILL NOT BE USED TO HORSES. YOU ARE URGENTLY REQUESTED TO RESPECT THIS FACT. PLEASE WALK WHEN NEAR TO OTHER USERS.

d House FM.

GREAT VERSDEN

Five Gables FM.

Church FM.

LITTLE EVERSDEN

g Close

Poultry FM.

Butlers Spinney

HARLTON

Roman Road

Eversden Quarry

Whole Way

Cracknow Hill

Orwell Road

BOXWORTH

**AN 11 MILE CIRCULAR TRAIL
(CLOCKWISE)**

Ordnance Survey Maps:
Landranger: 154
Pathfinder: 981

Parking & Starting Point:
From the A428 (formerly the A45)
turn for Knapwell (GR.335600). In
approximately one mile there is the
unmarked driveway and entrance to
New Farm, on the right hand side.
Just before this driveway there is a
wide verge which offers ample
parking.

*Please note that this spot is rather
isolated.*

Route Description:

From your parking point, continue
along the road towards Knapwell
village. Ride through the village
towards the Elsworth/Boxworth
crossroads. Cross the road and
continue riding for about one mile,
towards Conington.

1. Just before Conington village,
turn right (GR.325661) through the
gate into the field and follow the
waymarked bridleway. Please shut
the gate; there is livestock in the
field. Cross the narrow wooden
bridge with gates at either side and
follow the track with the hedge to
your left. Go through the metal
gate and continue along the side of
the field.

2. You will see two tall trees over
to your right. When you draw level

with these the track goes through a
gap in the hedge and you continue
to ride uphill on the grassy track
with the ditch and hedge to your
right. After 0.5 miles the track
turns left following the ditch, then
after 500 yards turn right onto the
farm track.

3. Ride past the barn on your left
and straight ahead on the farm
track to the crossroads (GR.
349646). Ride directly across into
Manor Lane following the waymark
to Lolworth. Ride past the houses
and into the field, following the
track where it bends to the right
and goes through Yarmouth Farm
and up the concrete track the other
side.

4. When you reach the High Street
in Lolworth, turn right and follow
the bridleway sign to Childerley.
The concrete track soon becomes a
wide grass path when you pass
Broadway Farm Stables. Follow this
track for about 1.5 miles and go
through the 5-barred gate and
along the side of the field keeping
the hedge to your right. You will
see a wooden gate ahead of you;
*ignore this as this is not your
route;* you should go through the
next gate to the left of the bushes.
Follow the track between the barns
to the left and turn right to join the
tarmac road.
Ride past Childerly Hall, where
Charles I was imprisoned by
Cromwell for one night. The site of
the mediaeval village is over to
your left.

5. After the left hand bend, you will see a bridleway 100 yards ahead on the right (GR.355615). Follow this across the field and around the edge of the next field towards Birds Pastures Farm.

6. Turn right onto the farm track (GR.346609) and follow this to turn left on to the track known as Thorofare Lane (GR.344623)*. Ride along this to its end in Knapwell (GR.333624). Turn left and ride away from the village and back to your parking place.

NB: Thorofare Lane is a very narrow path, which can be very boggy in wet weather and may be overgrown in the summer months. Should riders wish to avoid this section at the end of their trail, the alternative route is to continue along Battle Gate Road into Boxworth and turn left on reaching the High Street opposite the Golden Ball public house (GR. 344641). Ride to the crossroads (GR.326641) and turn left. Ride through Knapwell village and continue back to your parking spot.

Trail 18

HATLEY & GRANSDENS

A 12 MILE CIRCULAR TRAIL (CLOCKWISE)

Ordnance Survey Maps:
Landranger:
153
Pathfinders:
1003 & 1026

Parking & Starting Point:
Parking is available on the grass verge of the B1046, just past the old railway bridge (GR.298537), and before the Water Tower.

Of Interest:
This ride goes through Hayley Wood which is a Site of Special Scientific Interest (SSSI). This is a wet wood and has been a nature reserve since 1962. Please do not pick or collect any flowers, even common ones.

The wood dates back 800 years and is first mentioned by name in the Ely Coucher Book, a record of the possessions of the Bishop of Ely in 1251, and from this time its history is well documented. In 1365 the bishop of Ely was on the run for murder, and the king seized his estates. They were handed on to others until Queen Elizabeth I confiscated and sold the wood in 1602. It then passed through a long succession of owners before the Wildlife Trust purchased it.

You will find lots of butterflies and

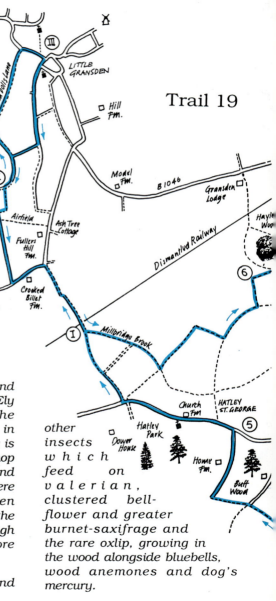

Trail 19

other insects which feed on valerian, clustered bell-flower and greater burnet-saxifrage and the rare oxlip, growing in the wood alongside bluebells, wood anemones and dog's mercury.

Route Description:

1. From your parking place, ride along the B1046 away from Longstowe towards the water tower. Turn left onto the bridleway that is opposite the water tower and ride into Hayley Wood. Follow

the track alongside the wood to the end (GR. 296527) and continue straight ahead on the grass bridleway that is in front of you. Ride along here until you come to a stony track (GR.297525) and turn right along it. After about 100 yards, past the barns to your right, take the bridleway to the left along the side of the field.

2. On reaching a farm track (GR.299522) ride straight ahead, in a southerly direction for about 1.5 miles keeping to the farm track until you come into Manor Farm (GR.312498). The bridleway takes you through the farm yard, past the church, then into Croydon village.

3. When you join the High Street (GR. 317496), turn right and ride through the village. After .75 miles cross Larkins Road (GR.306491) and continue along the bridleway directly ahead. *This is part of the Clopton Way and your route now takes you past the site of the Medieval village of Clopton.* **Follow this bridleway as it runs parallel to the A603. There may be livestock along this bridleway so please close any gates that you open along this part of the trail.**

4. Here you have a choice of route, either: a) Turn right (GR.292485) onto the definitive bridleway which is the farm track to Top Farm (*NB. there are private aircraft here*), and ride with care through the farm yard turning right

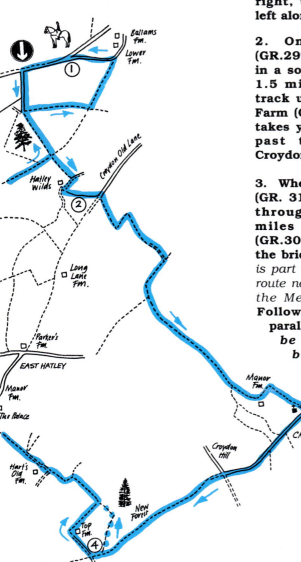

(GR.290488) and continuing to a junction of bridleways (GR.294490).

or: b) Take the attractive permissive path which avoids the farm yard. If you wish to take this option, follow the permissive markers and ride in a north easterly direction with the ditch to your right, heading towards the small copse, 'New Forest'. Turn left (GR.296488) and ride on to join the definitive route (GR.294490). Take care here that there are no aircraft using the airfield. Follow this public bridleway towards Buff Wood (GR.283501).

NB. The definitive route between Top Farm (GR.290488) and Harts Old Farm (GR.288487) has been diverted east of its original line, to a new line around field edges. This will differ slightly to that shown on your Ordnance Survey map.

At Buff Wood, the trail continues along the track between the wood, which is to your right and the barn, to your left. Follow the track and then turn right (GR.279503) onto Buff Lane and follow the lane to Hatley St George.

5. On reaching the High Street, turn left and ride through the village. Turn onto the third bridleway on the right (GR. 273515). Continue to a T-junction of bridleways (GR.270523)*. *If you wish to extend your ride by 5 miles at this point then follow the instructions given at the end of the route description.* If not, then continue as follows:

Turn right and continue along the bridleway with Millbridge Brook to your right. Turn left (GR.276518) uphill, and then turn right (GR.281521). After 500 yards turn left and follow the grass track until it meets the concrete track (GR.288523). Turn left and ride downhill towards the barn.

6. Turn right by the barn and ride past the wood which is on your left, across the wooden bridge and turn left (GR.295527), ride alongside the wood. Halfway along this track there is an opening to the right (GR.294533). Turn onto this path and follow it until it turns left (GR.300531), by a wooden fence. At the end of the next field (GR.304536) turn left onto the wide grass track and ride over the old railway bridge back to your starting point.

Riders wishing to ride the additional 5 miles at (GR.270523) should follow the following route:

i) Take the left hand bridleway (GR.270523) across the disused railway line, and ride up to meet the road at Fullers Hill (GR.267531). Turn left and after 500 yards turn right onto the bridleway through the trees.

NB Take care as you emerge from the trees to look both ways as the bridleway is crossed by a runway used by light aircraft! Ride directly across, through the gap in the hedge, and immediately turn right. Continue around the edge of the field turning left.

ii) Turn right onto the farm track (GR.264540) and follow this towards Waresly Wood. Continue along the bridleway around the edge of Waresley Wood and continue as the track bends right (GR.264547) and becomes Dick and Dolls bridleway, which you follow into Little Gransden. At the end of the bridleway turn right and ride along the road.

iii) Turn right into Church Street (GR.271553). This is a 'No Through Road' which then becomes a grass bridleway. Continue to turn right (GR.269543) and then left (GR.265543) and follow the farm track to turn left (GR.263549) onto the field edge path. *You are now approaching the aircraft runway that you crossed earlier.*

Turn left (GR.263547) taking care to look for any light aircraft. Continue directly ahead through the trees until you meet the road (GR.264590). Turn left and after 500 yards turn right on to the bridleway which then takes you

back across the disused railway line. Continue to a T-junction of bridleways (GR.270523). Take the left hand bridleway and continue riding with Millbridge Brook to your right. *You now rejoin the main route.*

Turn left (GR.276518) uphill and turn right (GR.281521). After 500 yards turn left and follow the grass track until it meets the concrete track (GR.288523). Turn left and ride downhill towards the barn.

Turn right by the barn and ride past the wood which is on your left, across the wooden bridge to turn left (GR.295527). Ride alongside the wood. Halfway along this track (GR.293533) there is an opening to the right, turn onto this path and follow it until it turns left (GR.300531) by a wooden fence. At the end of the next field (GR.304536) turn left onto the wide grass track and ride over the old railway bridge back to your starting point.

THE BRITISH HORSE SOCIETY

The British Horse Society was founded in 1947 when two separate equestrian bodies - The National Horse Association and the Institute of the Horse and Pony Club - decided to join forces and work together for the good of both horse and rider.

It is a marriage that has proved to be a great success and the British Horse Society has steadily increased its membership from just 4000 in the late 1960's to over 60,000 in the 1990's.

By becoming members of the British Horse Society, horse lovers know they are joining a body of people with a shared interest in the horse. Members can be sure that they are contributing to the work of an equine charity with a primary aim to improve the standards of care for horses and ponies. Welfare is not only about the rescuing of horses in distress (which we do); it is also about acting to prevent abuse in the first place. There are many means to achieving this: by teaching and advising, by looking to the horse's well-being and safety, by providing off-road riding, by encouraging high standards in all equestrian establishments, and fighting for the horse's case with government and in Europe.

The British Horse Society works tirelessly towards these aims thanks to the work of its officials at Stoneleigh and its army of dedicated volunteers out in the field.

Membership benefits the horse lover as well as the horse; the Society can offer something to all equestrians, whether they are weekend riders, interested spectators or keen competitors. The benefits include free Third Party Public Liability and Personal Accident insurance, free legal advice, free publications, reductions to British Horse Society events, special facilities at the major shows, and free advice and information on any equine query.

Largely financed by its membership subscriptions, the Society welcomes the support of all horse lovers. If you are thinking of joining the Society and would like to find out more about our work, please contact the Membership Department at the following address:

The British Horse Society
British Equestrian Centre
Stoneleigh Park
Kenilworth
Warwickshire
CV8 2LR
(Telephone: 01203 696697)
Registered Charity No. 210504